MW01058919

101
WAYS TO KILL A
ZOMBIE

Robb Pearlman

Illustrations by Dave Urban

UNIVERSE

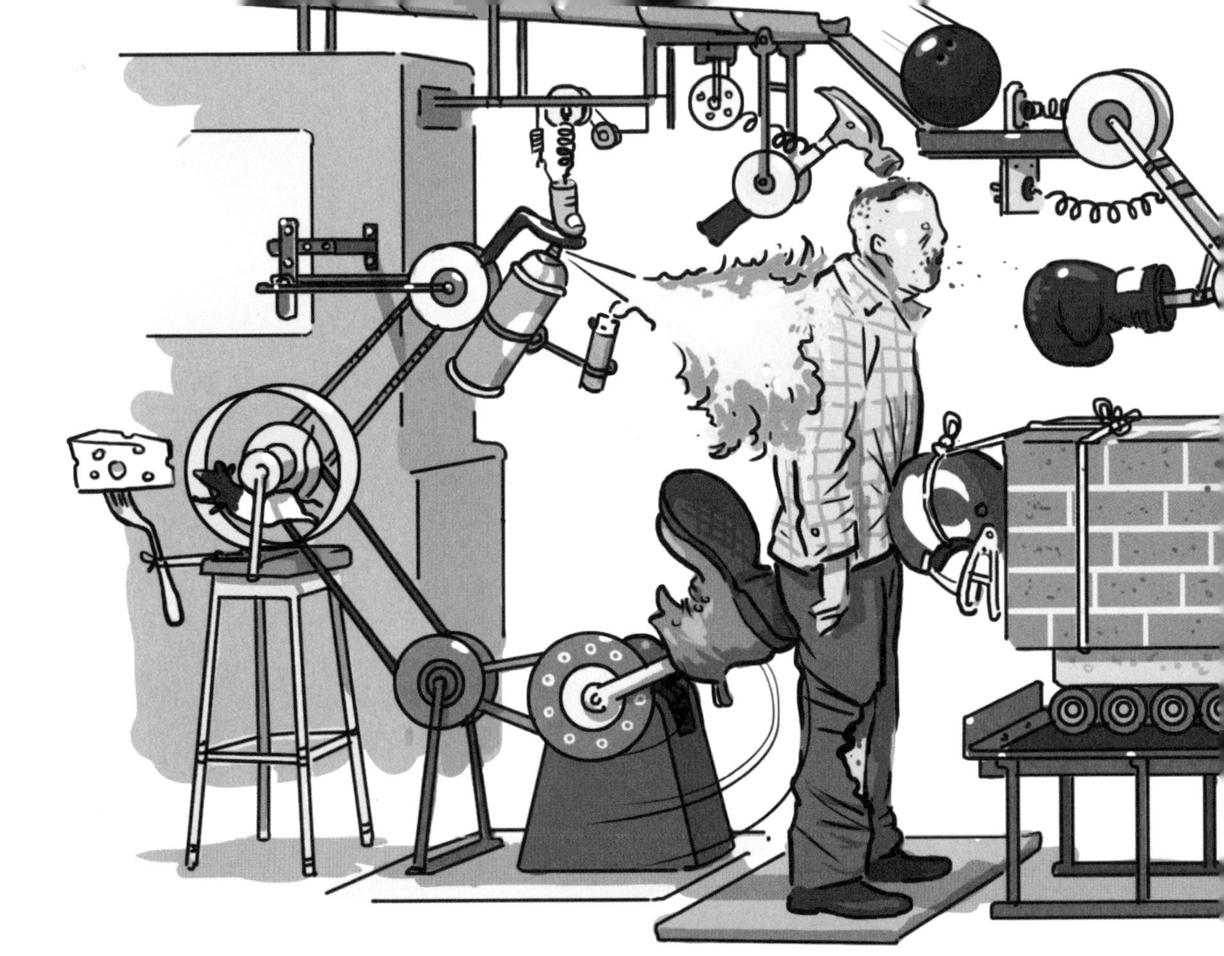

#1: Rube Goldberg–like

#2: Knife

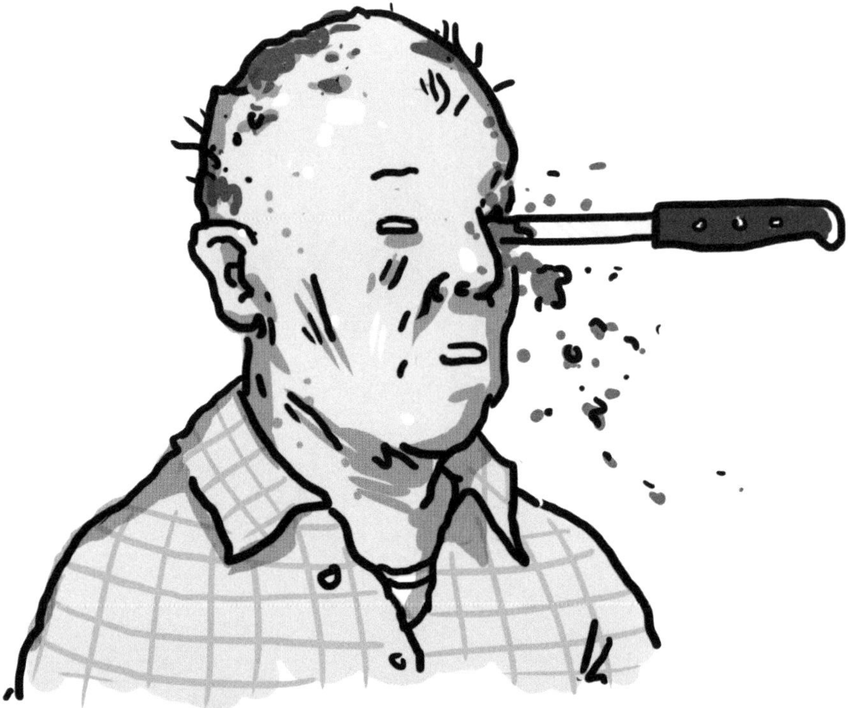

#3: Evisceration

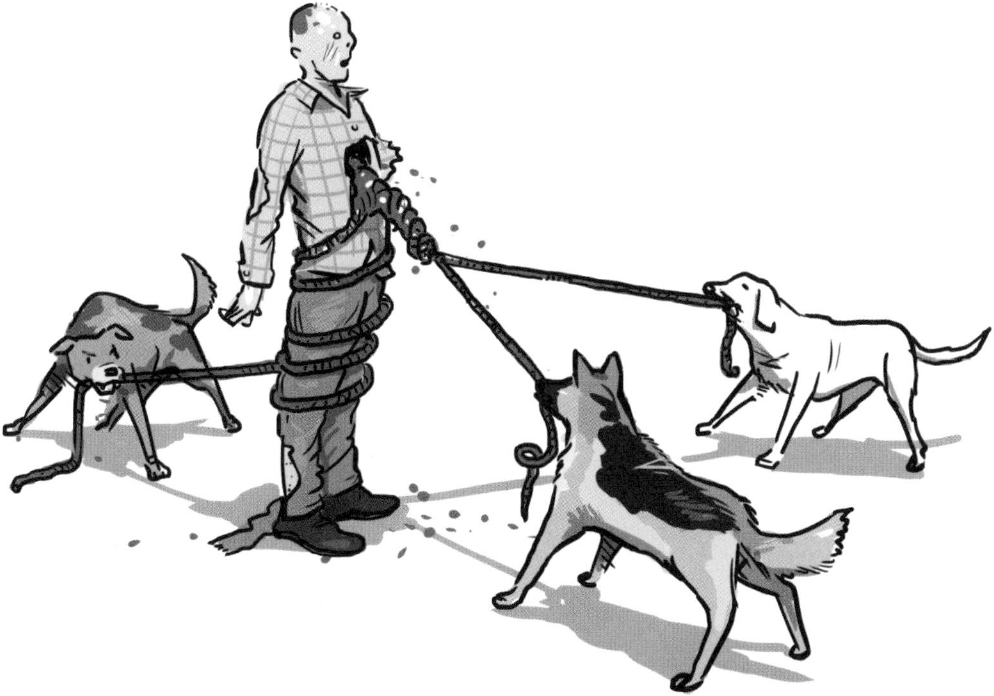

#4: Ax

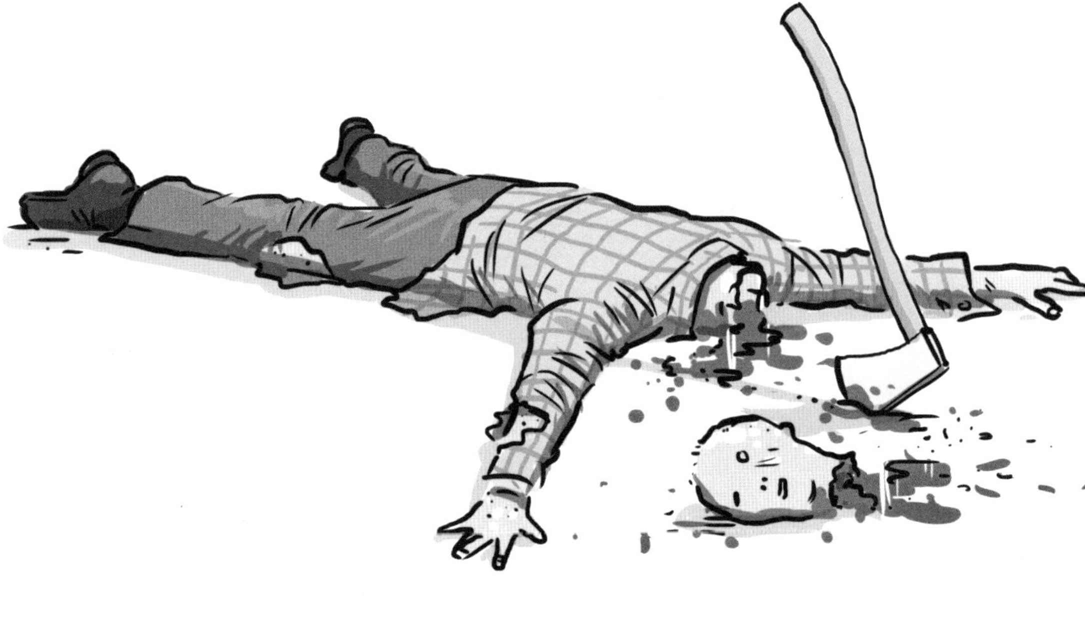

#5: AXE®

#6: Tanning Bed

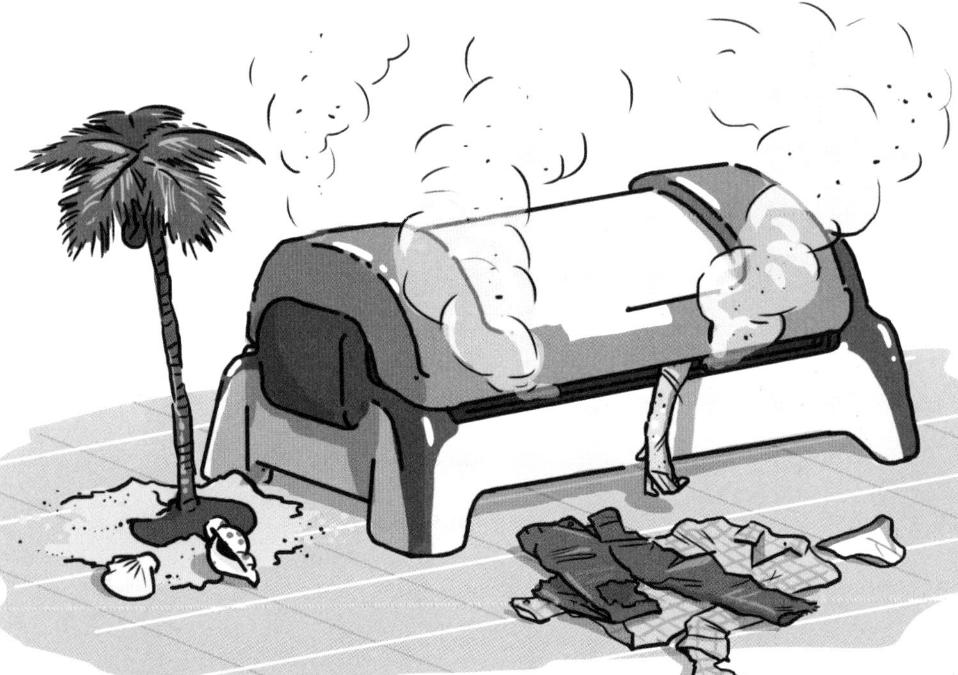

#7: Password Reset

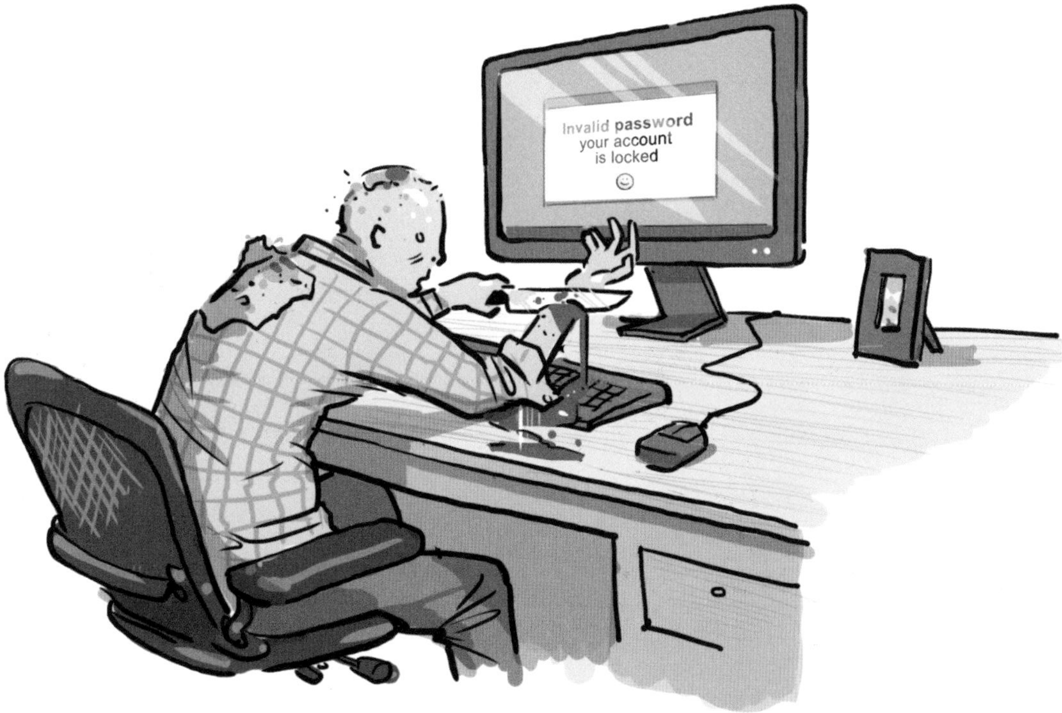
Invalid password
your account
is locked

#8: Overboard

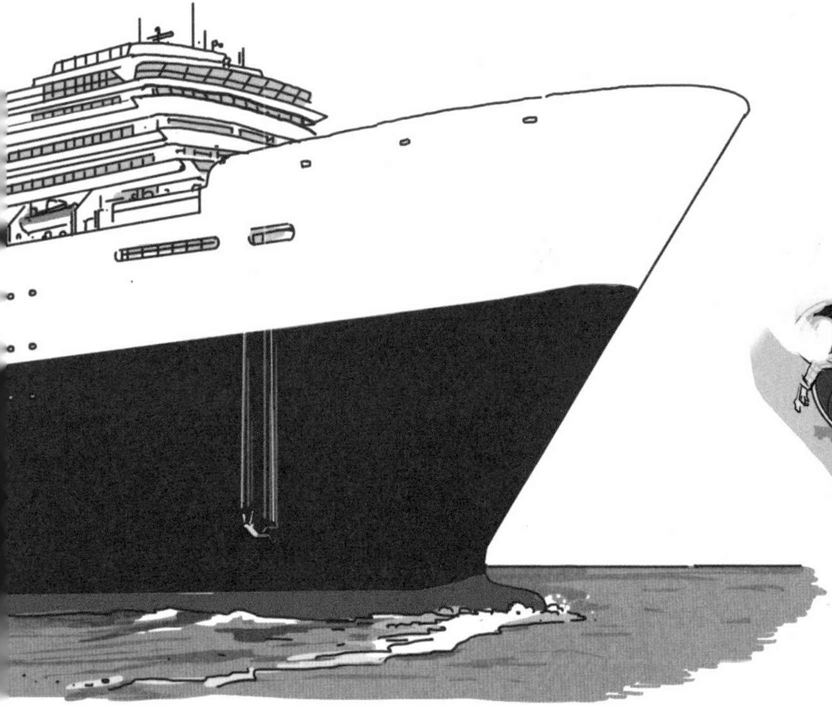

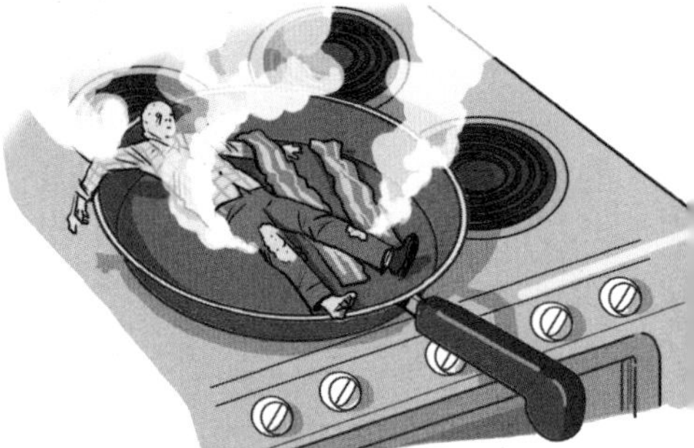

#9: Over Easy

#10: Ren Faire

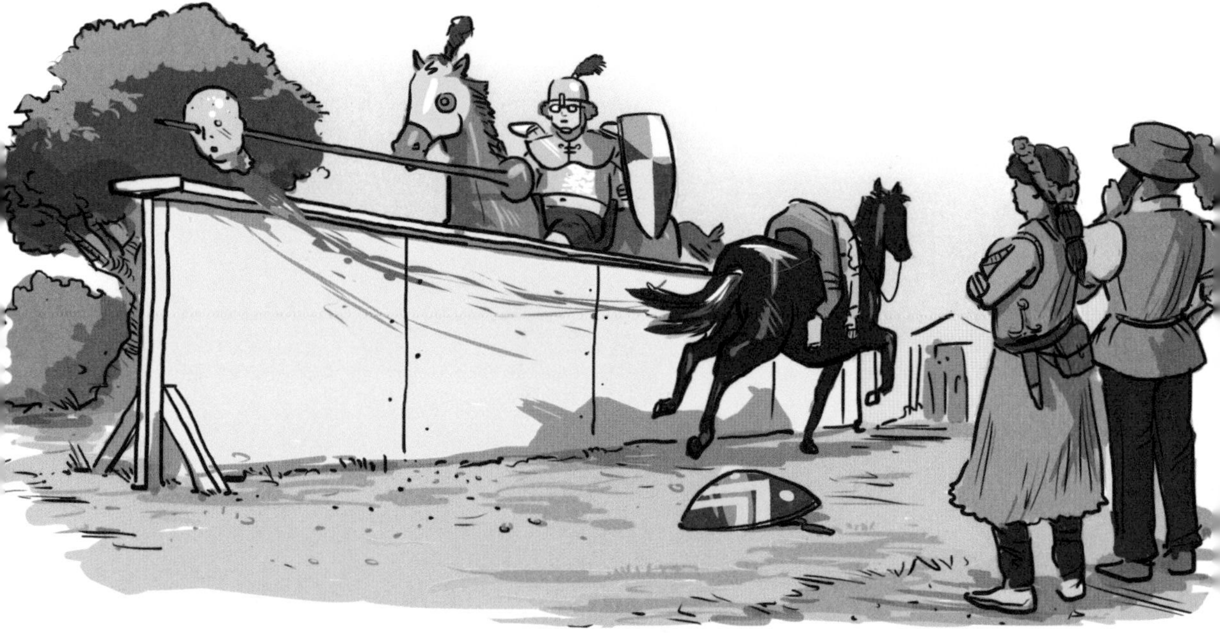

#11: Vacuum

#12: Vacuum

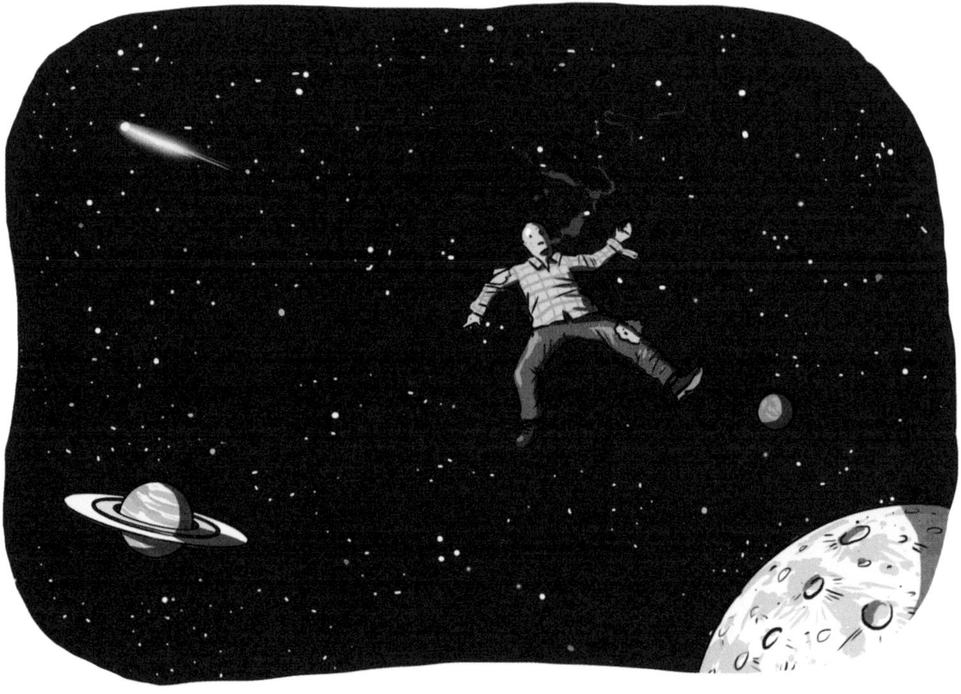

#13: Poodles

#14: Microwave

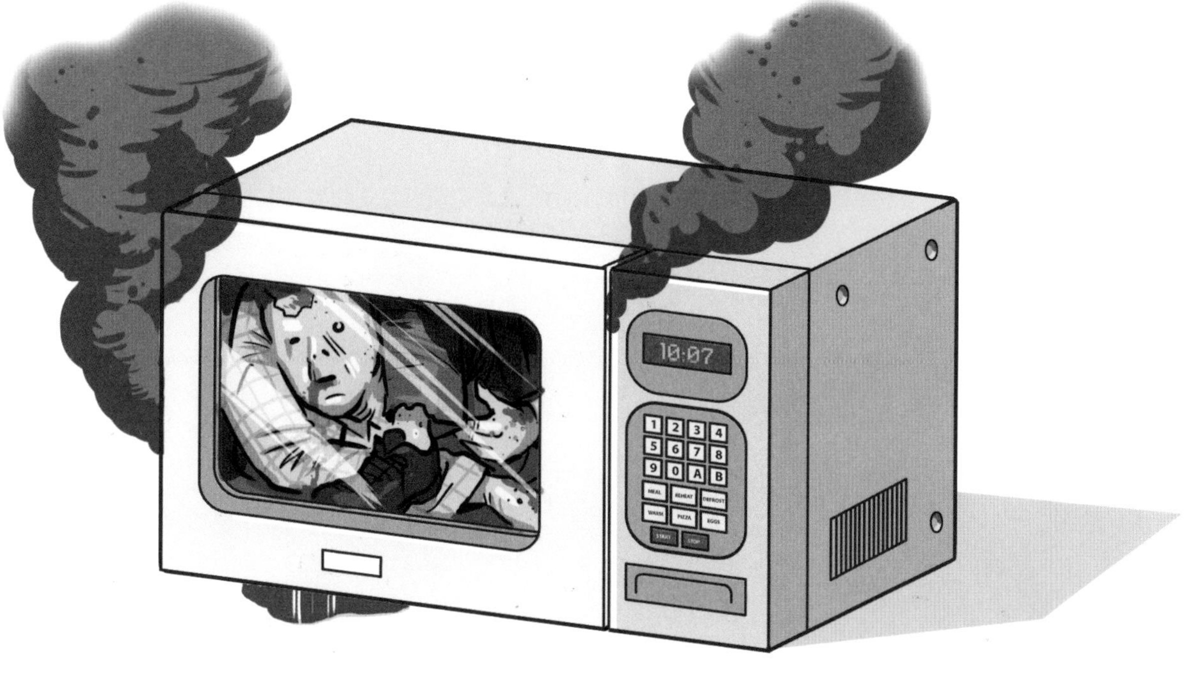
10:07
1 2 3 4
5 6 7 8
9 0 A B

#15: Brain Freeze

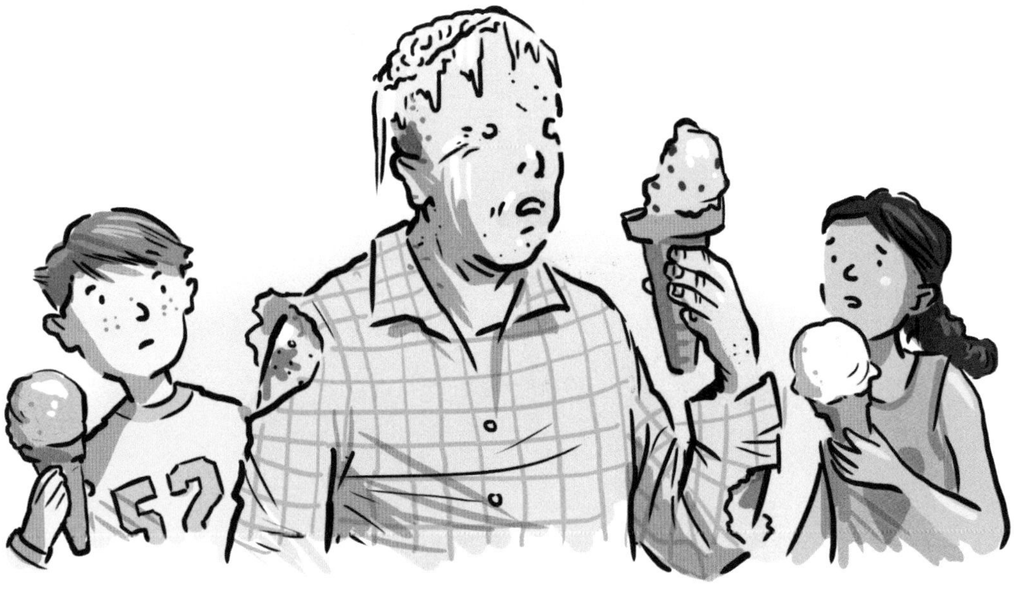
52

#16: Burning Man

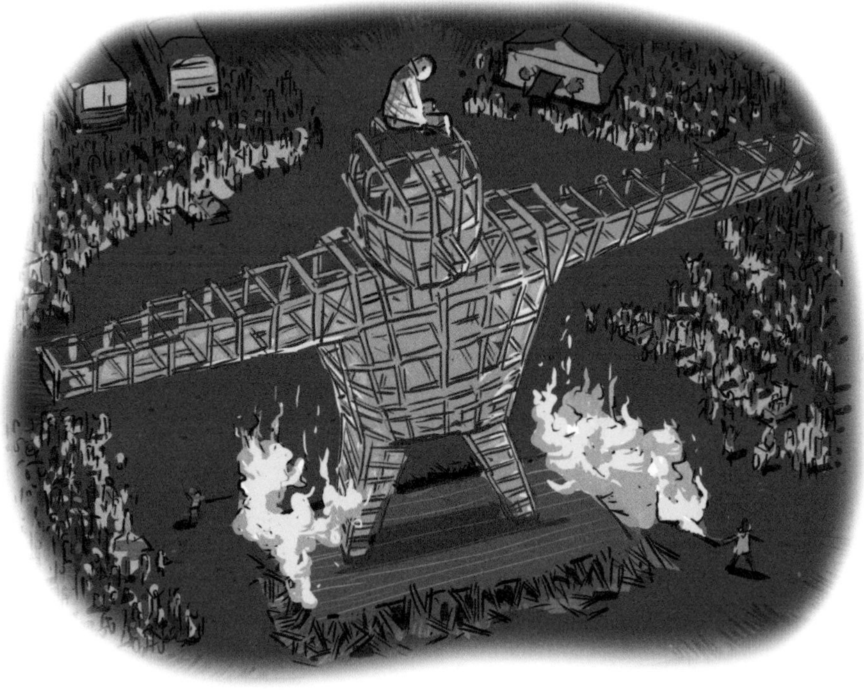

#17: Skinny Jeans

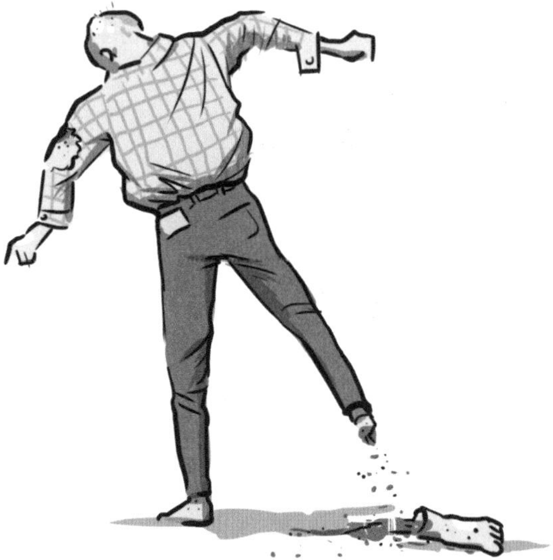

#18: Kindness

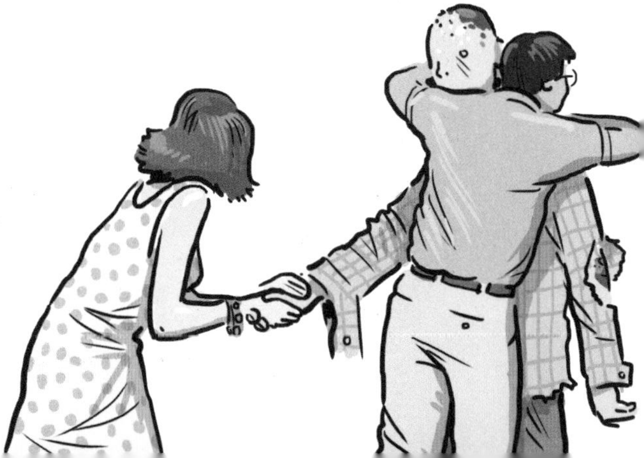

#19: Guillotine

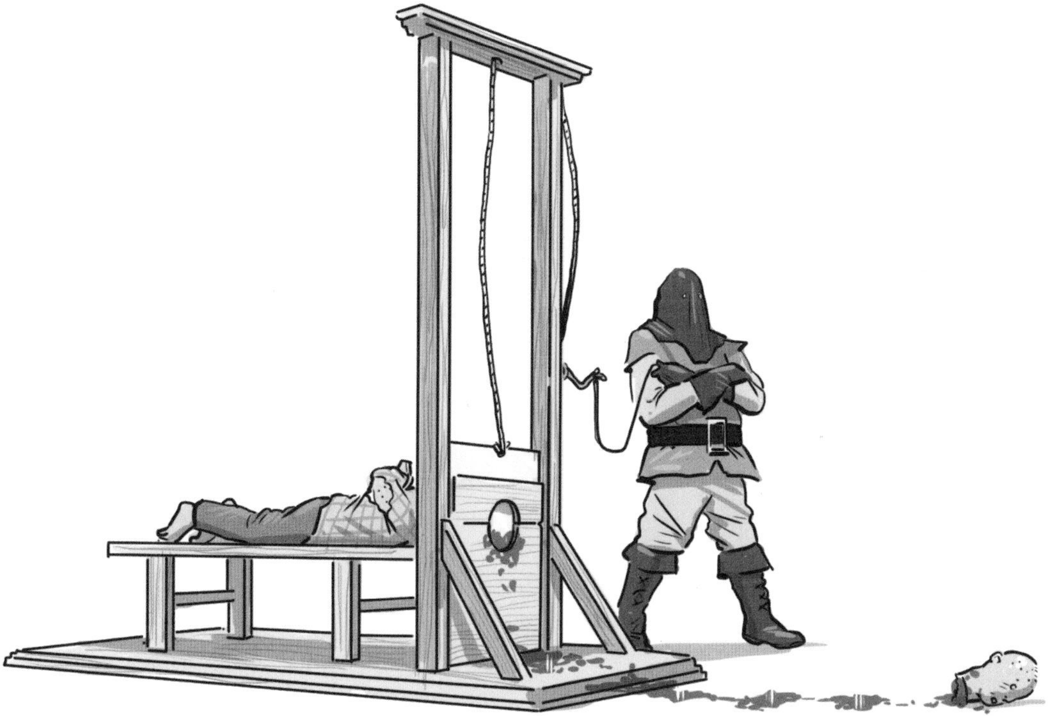

#20: Locusts

#21: WASPs

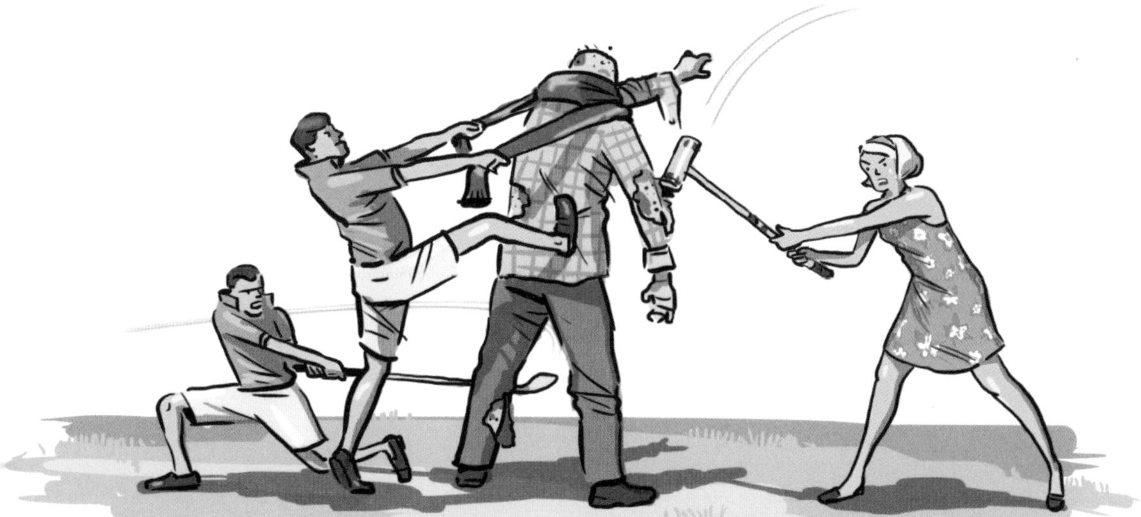

#22: Cricket

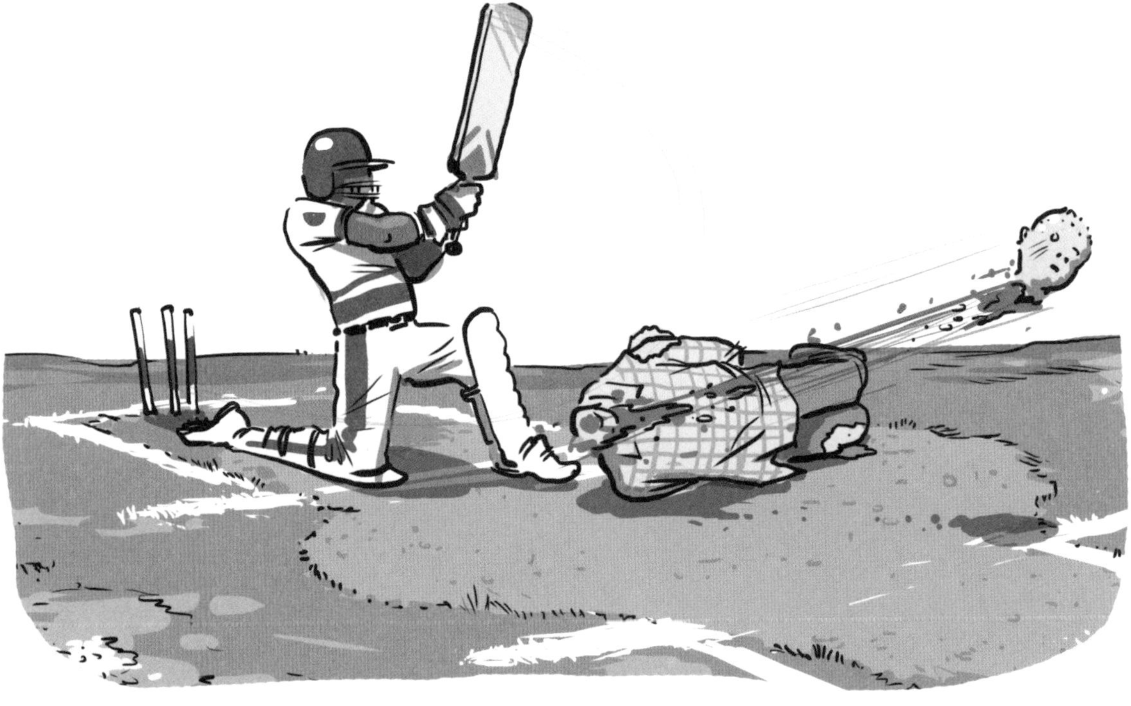

#23: Jiminy Cricket

#25: Screwdriver

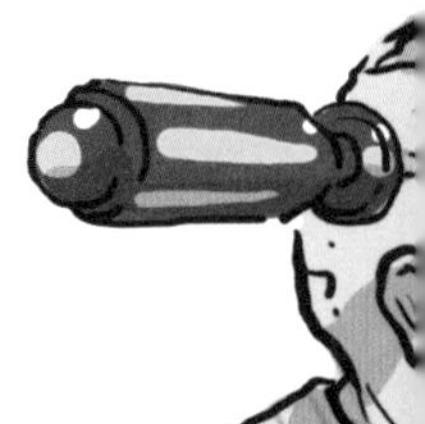

#24: Fireworks

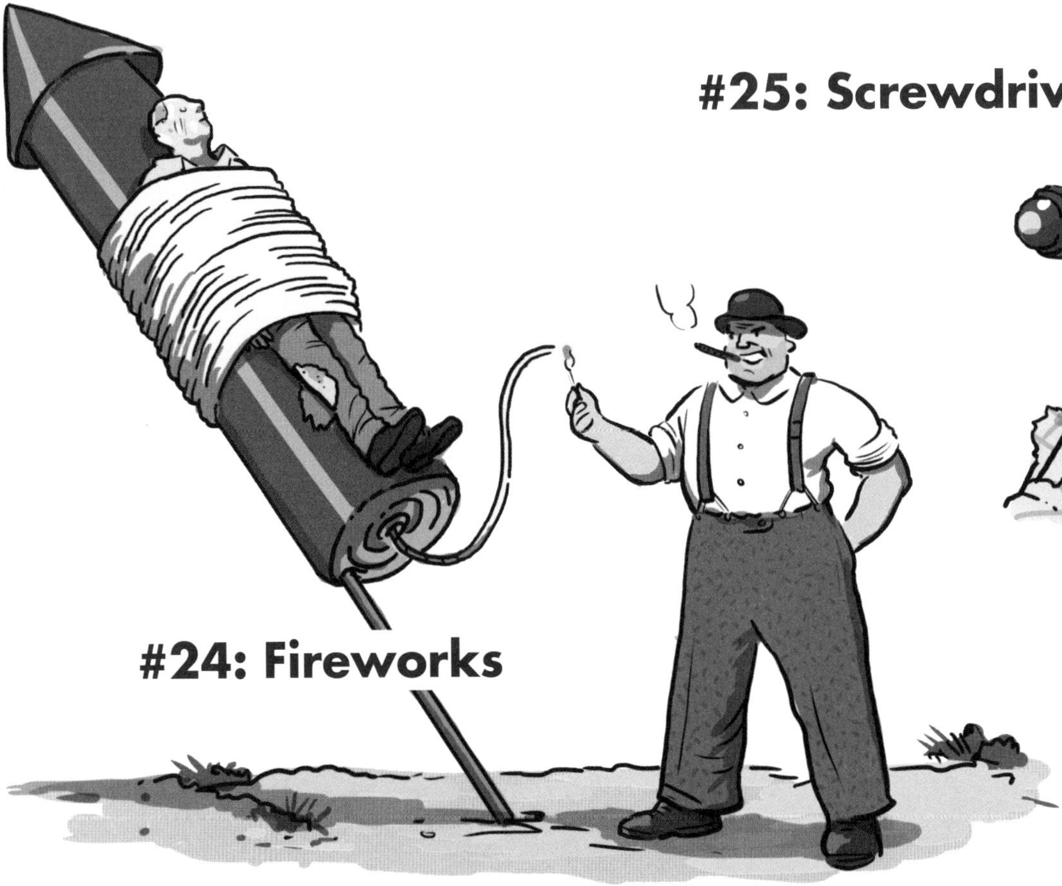

#26: Catapult

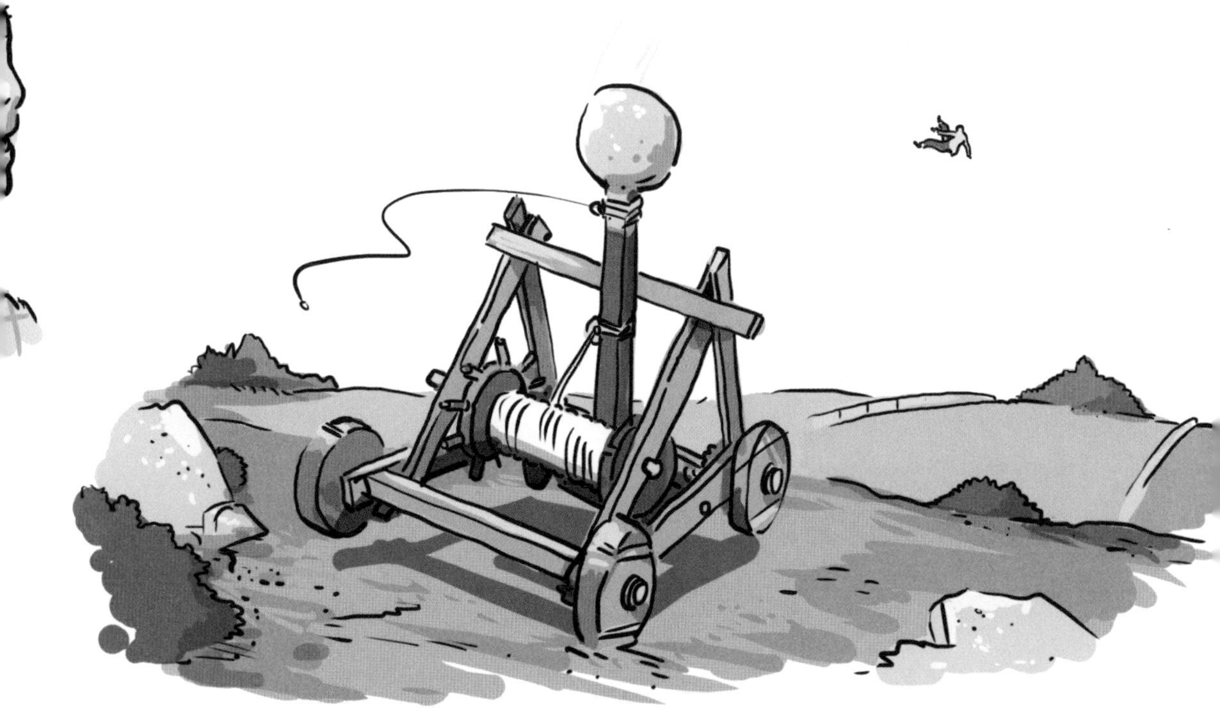

#27: Earworm

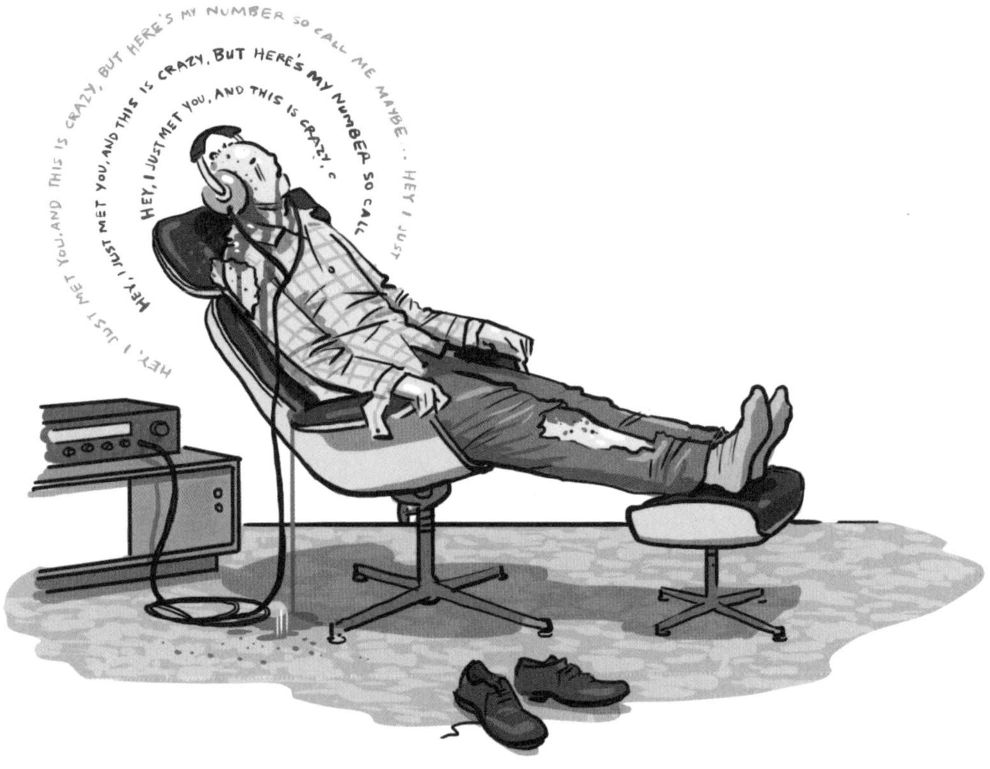
HEY, I JUST MET YOU. AND THIS IS CRAZY, BUT HERE'S MY NUMBER SO CALL ME MAYBE... HEY I JUST
HEY, I JUST MET YOU, AND THIS IS CRAZY, BUT HERE'S MY NUMBER SO CALL
HEY, I JUST MET YOU, AND THIS IS CRAZY, c

#28: T-Ball

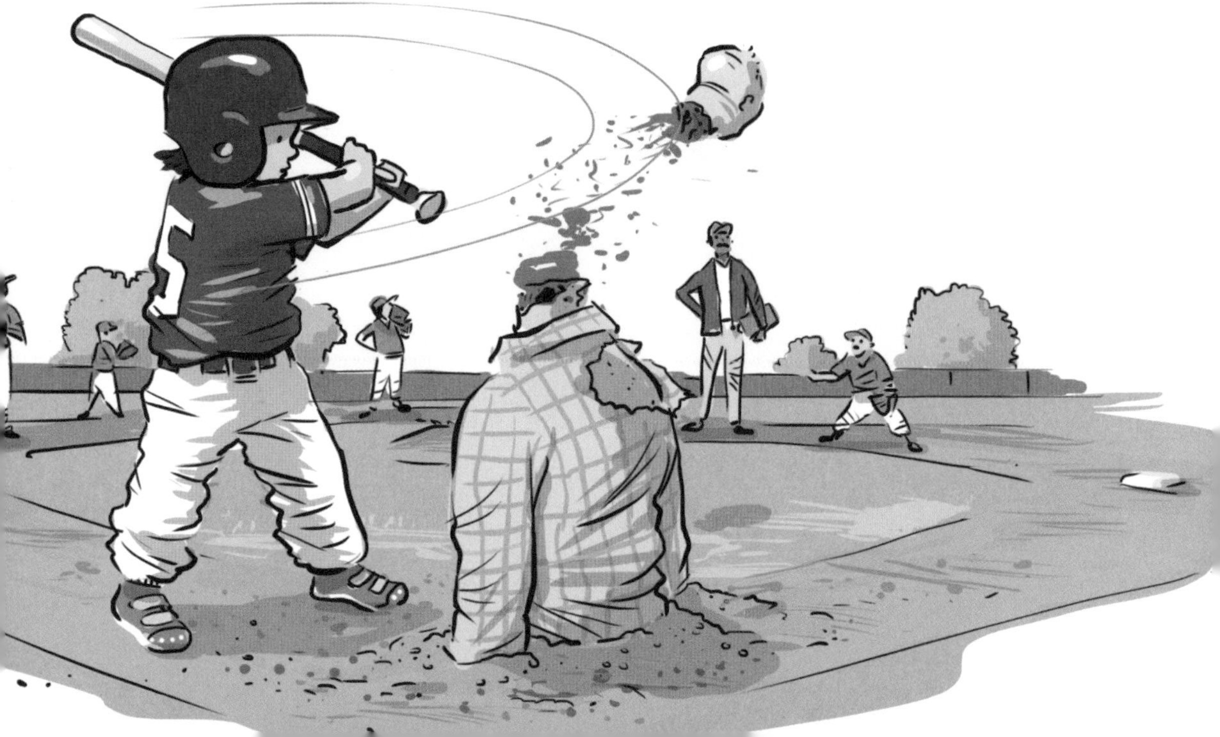

#29: T-Shirt Cannon

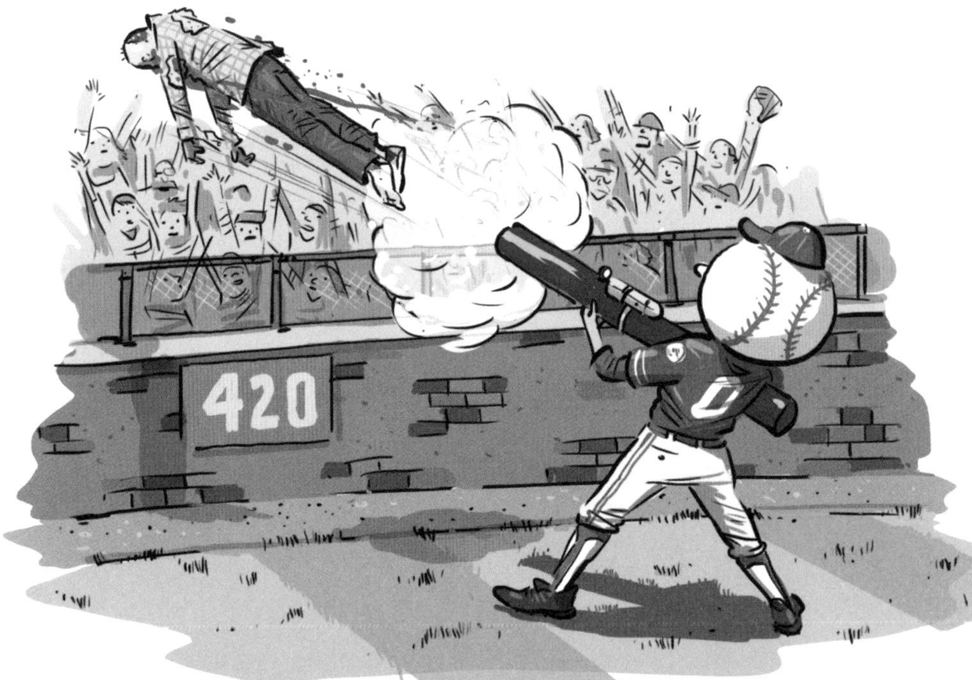
420

#30: Cannon

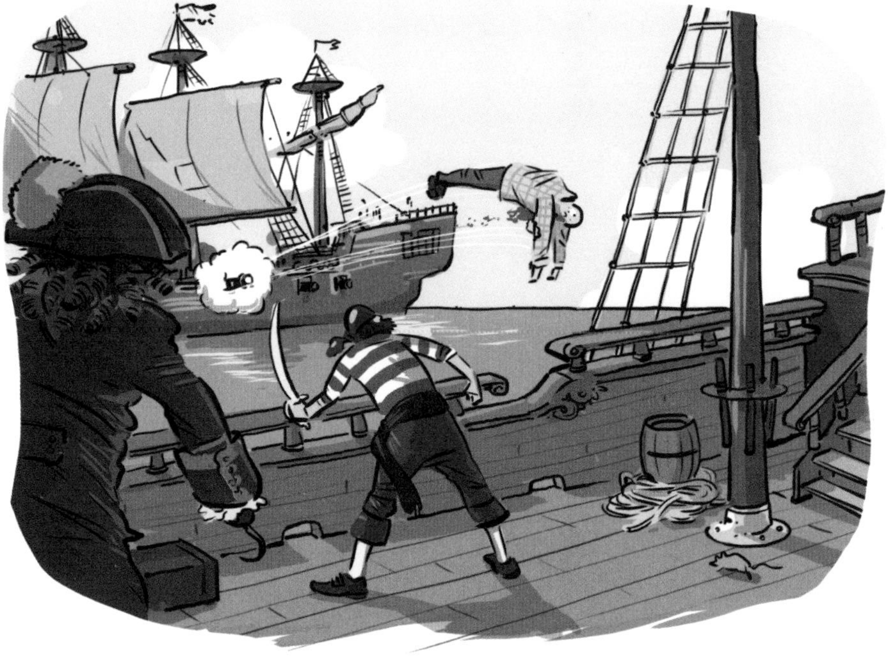

#31: Ninjas

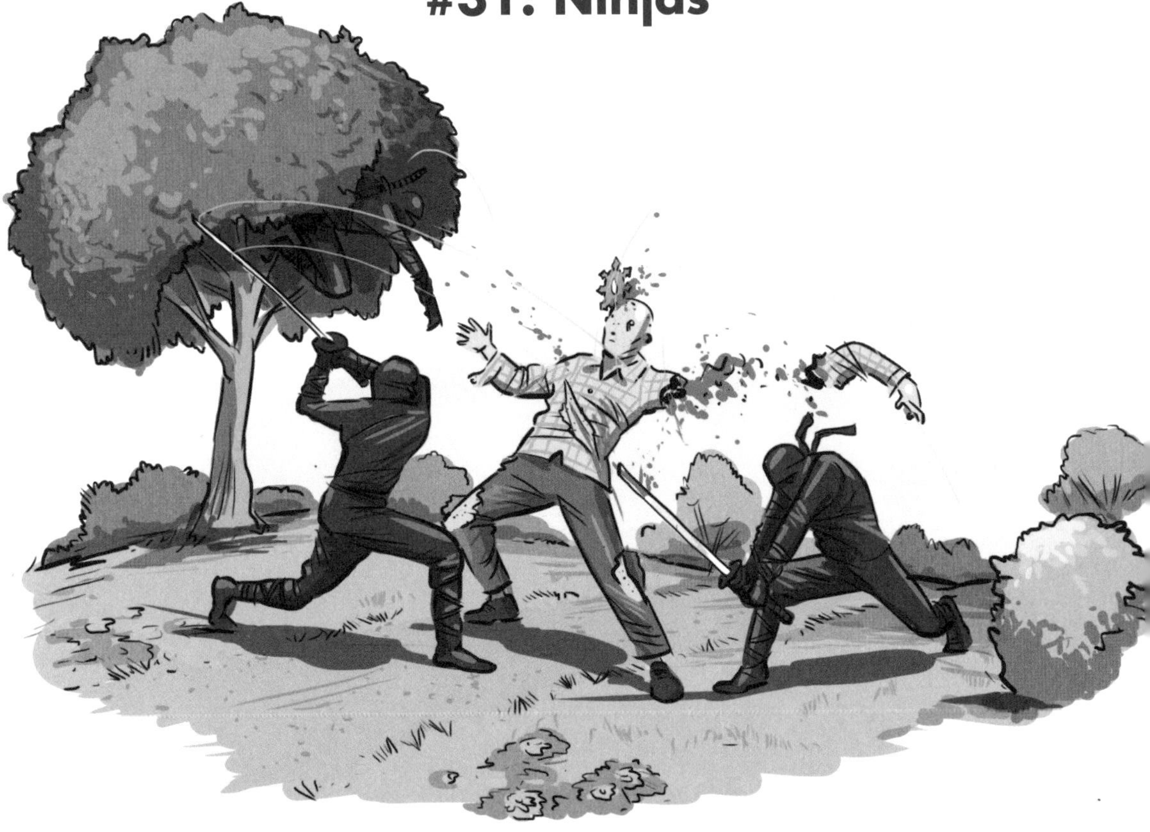

#32: Spin Cycle

#33: Flushing

#34: Iceberg

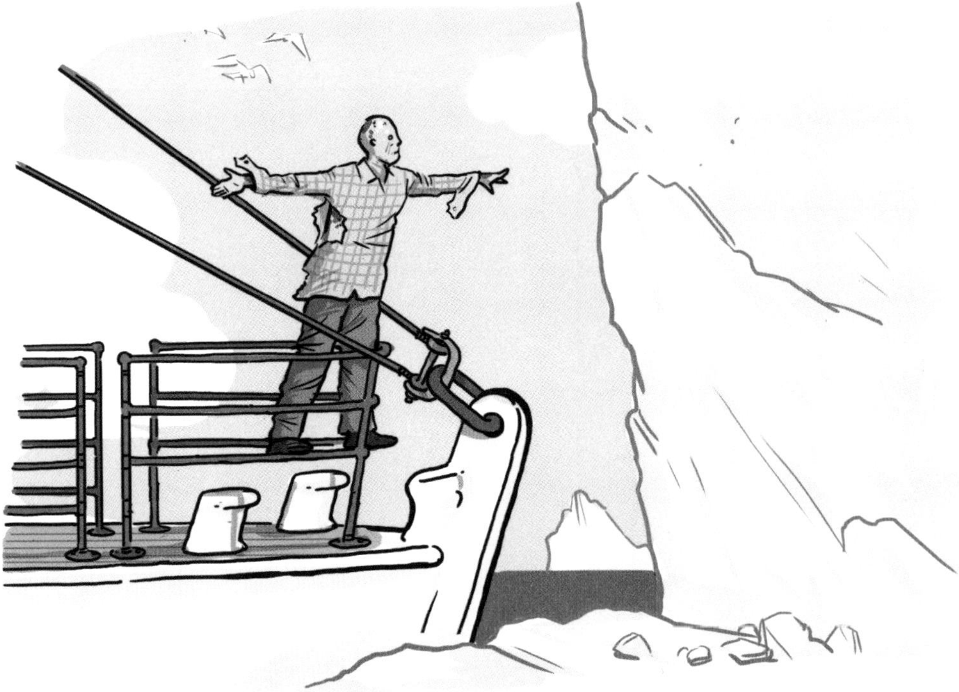

#35: Ice Pick

#36: Helping a Friend Move

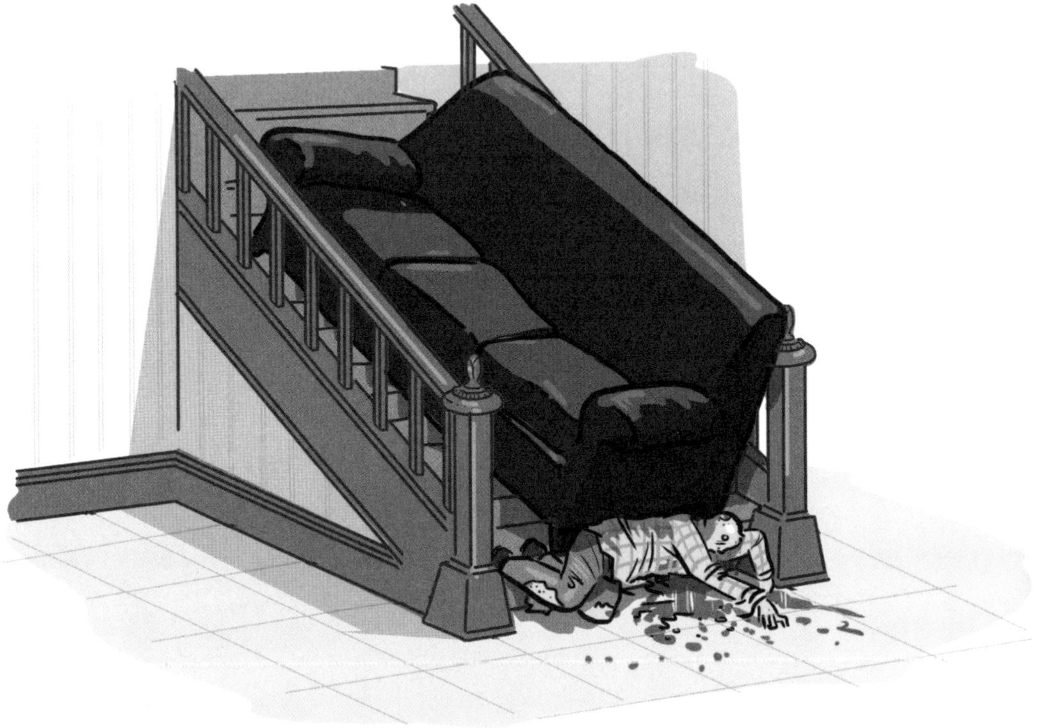

#37: Hot Dog Eating Contest

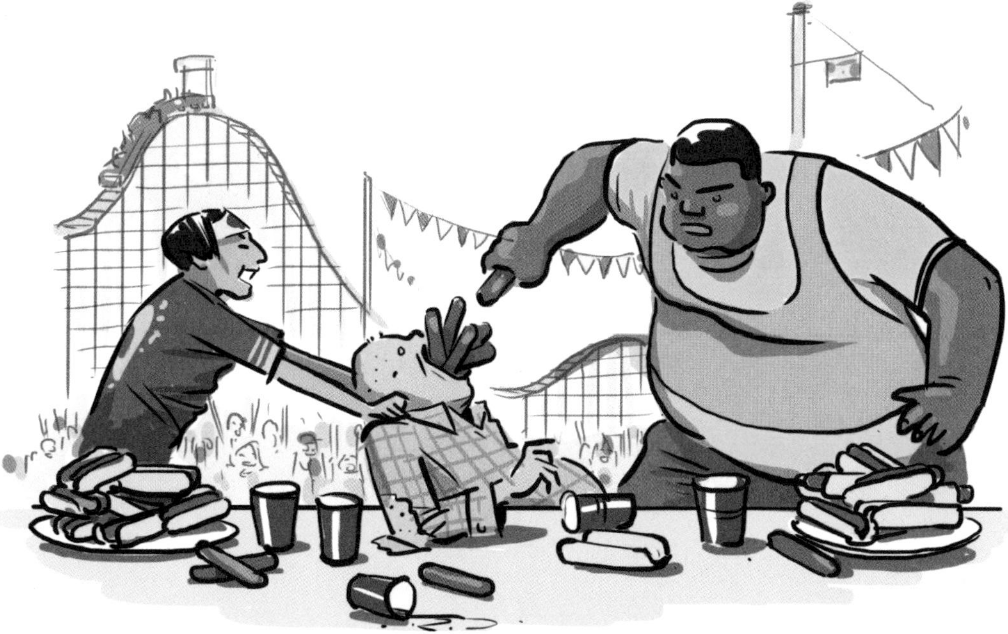

#38: Single White Femaled

#39: Spoilers

#40: Tuna Fishing

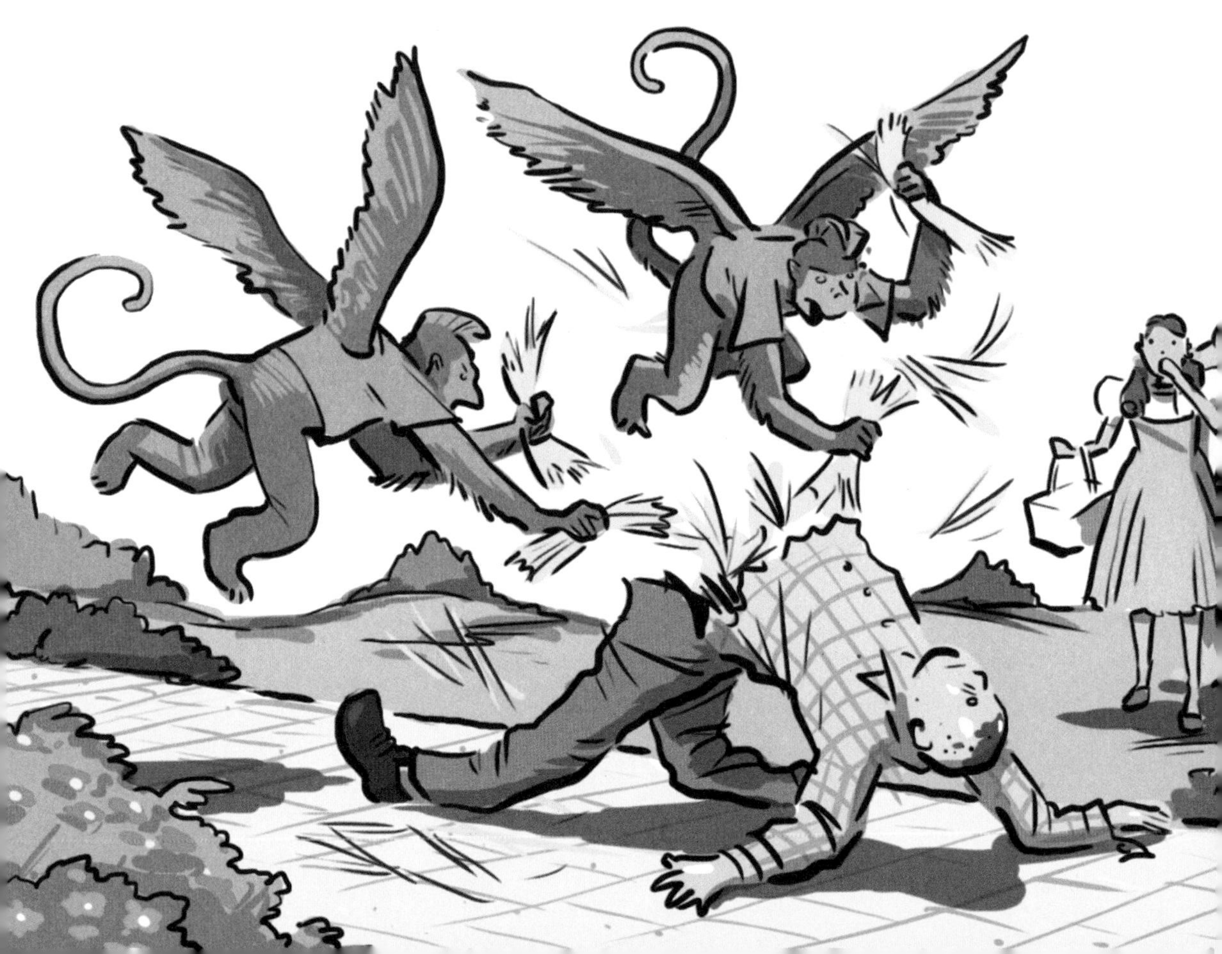

#41: Flying Monkeys

#42: Willy Wonka Factory Tour

#43: Poison Apple

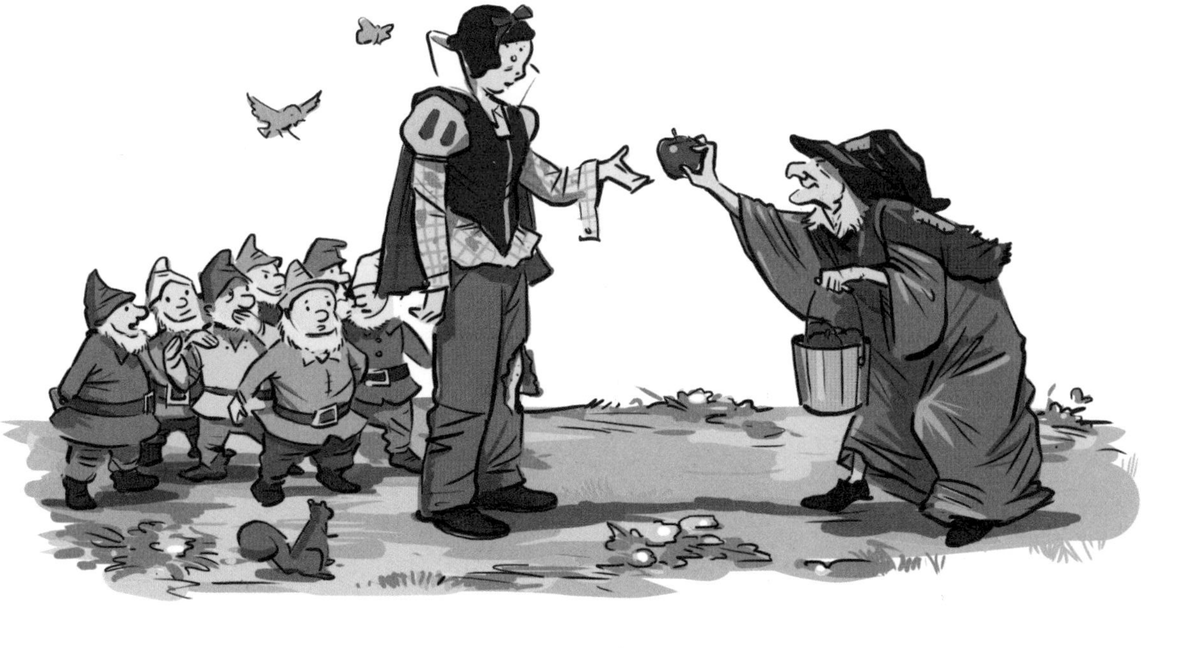

#44: Nerd Rage

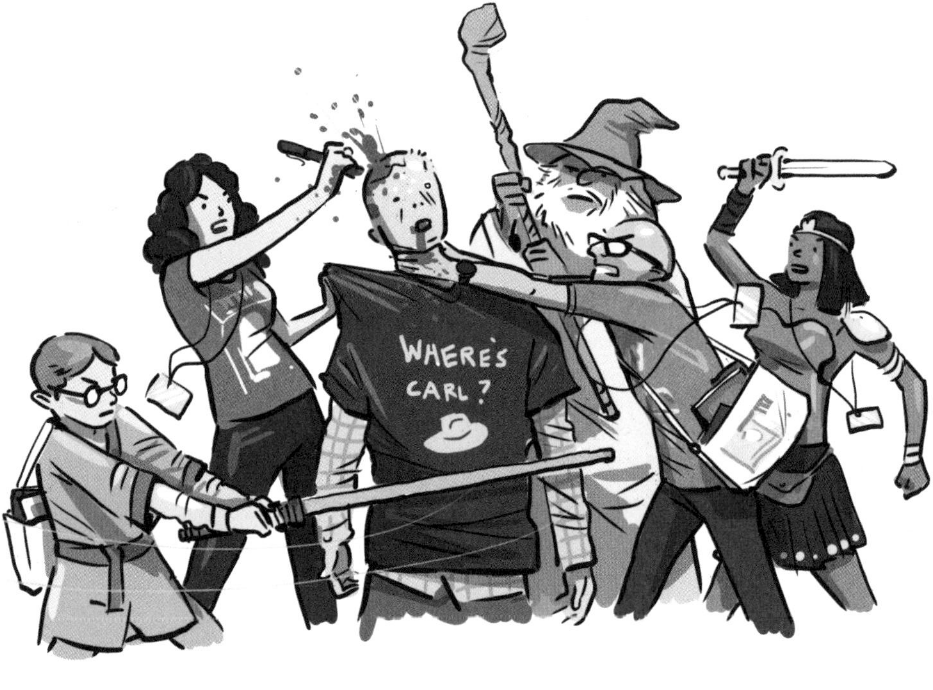
WHERE'S
CARL?

#45: Vacation Photos

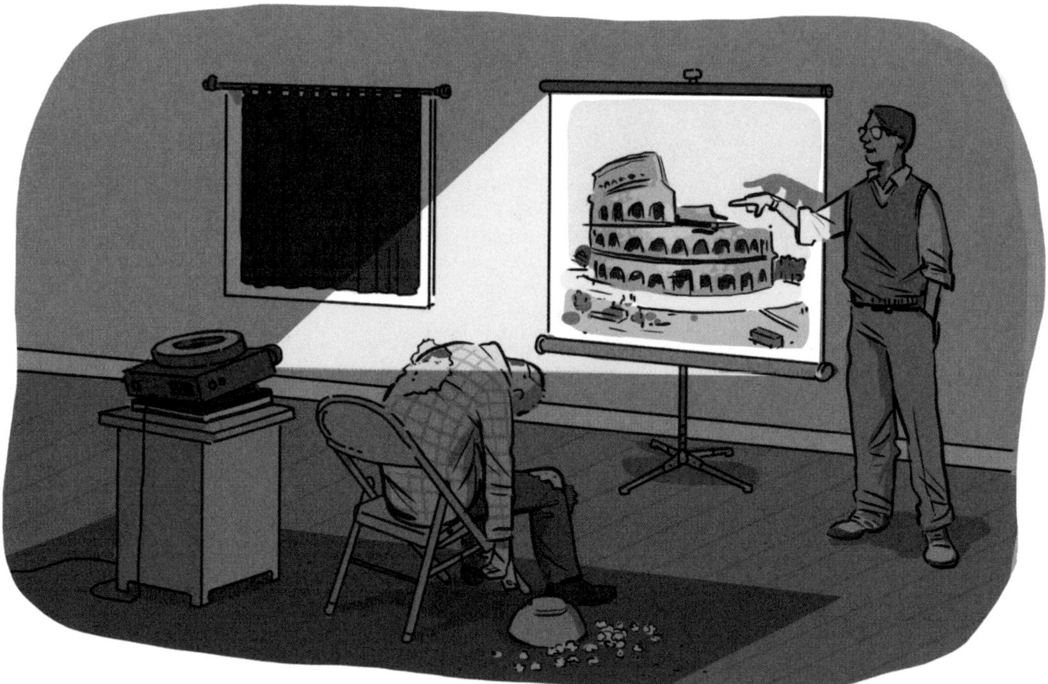

#46: Electrocution

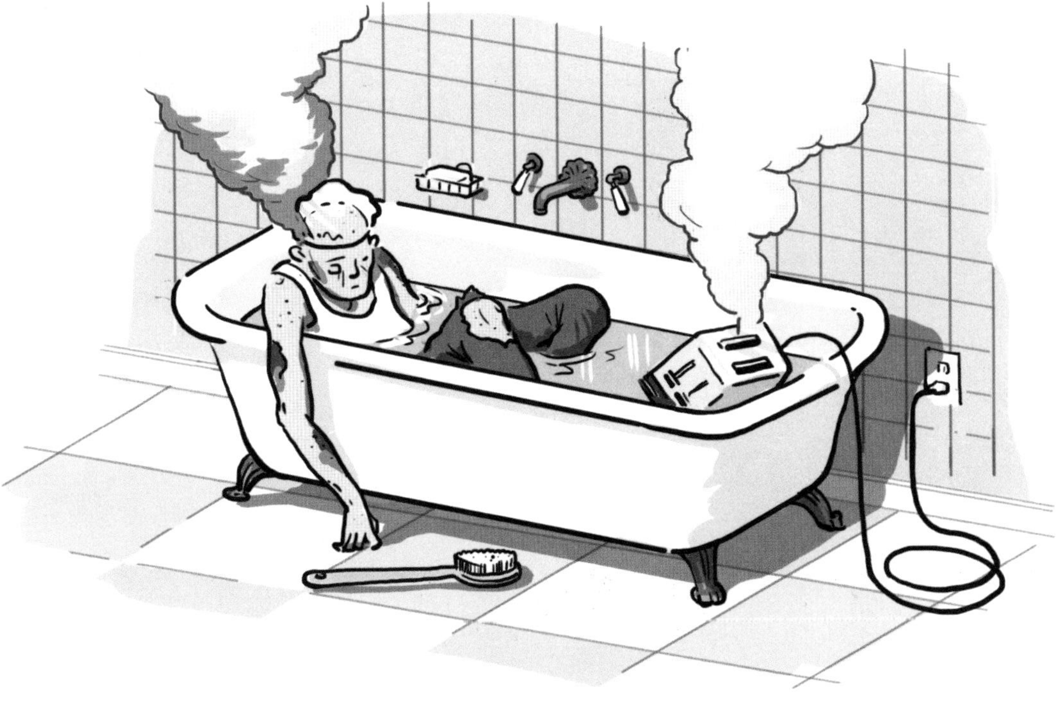

#47: Crossbow

#48: Cross-Training

#49: Mosh Pit

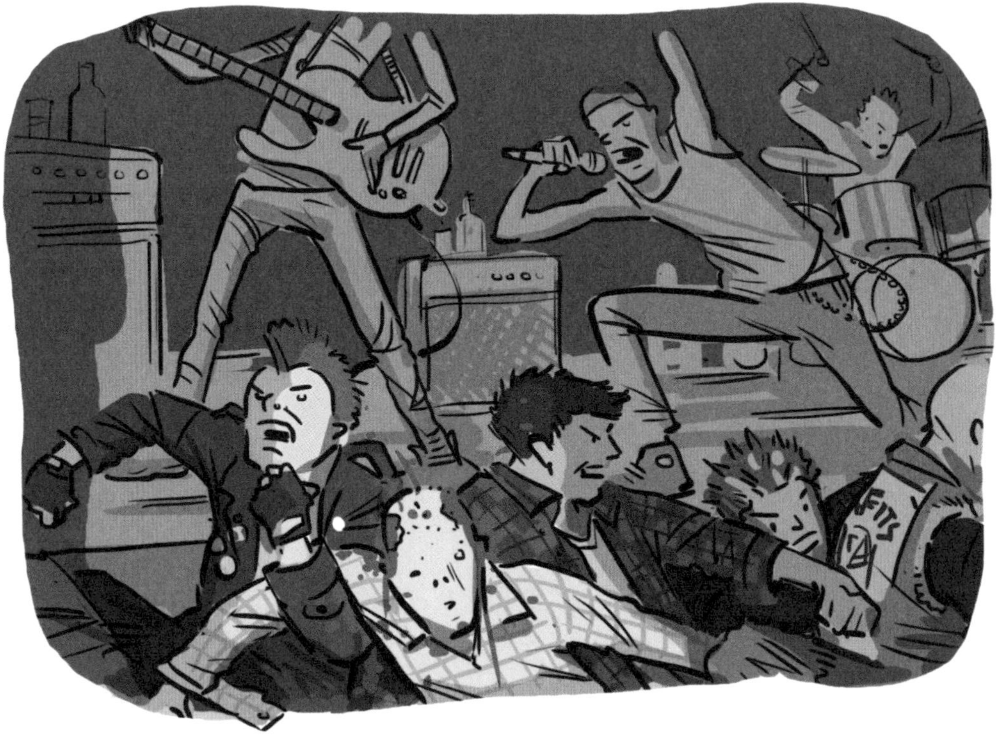

#50: Hindenberging

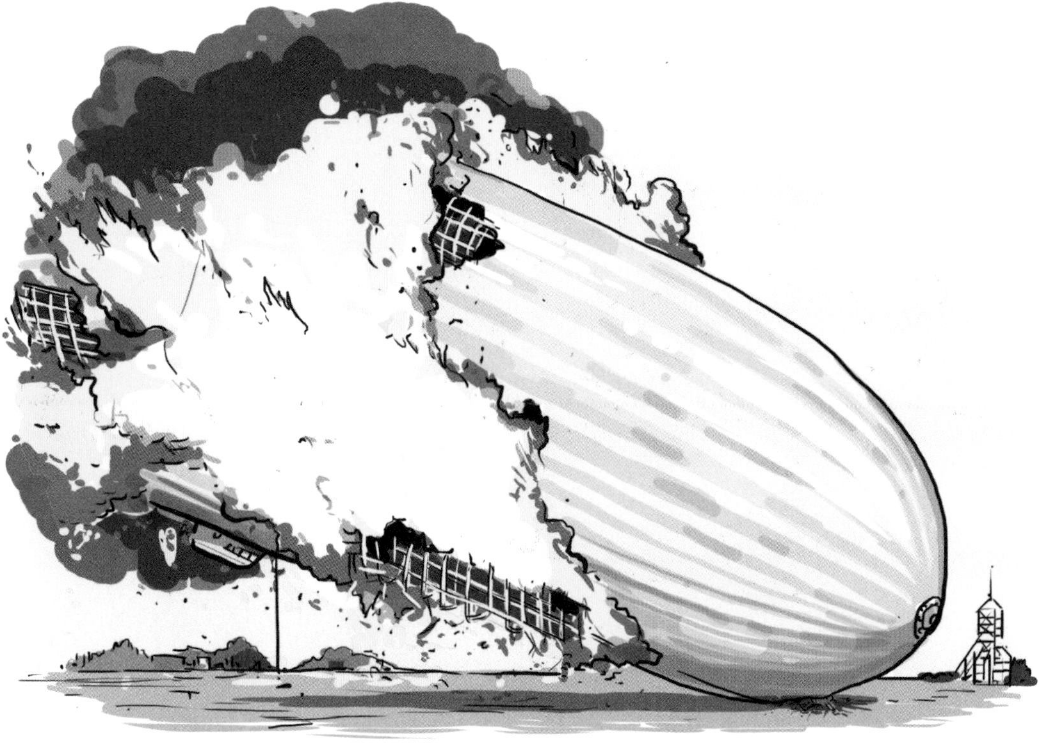

#51: Brazilian Wax

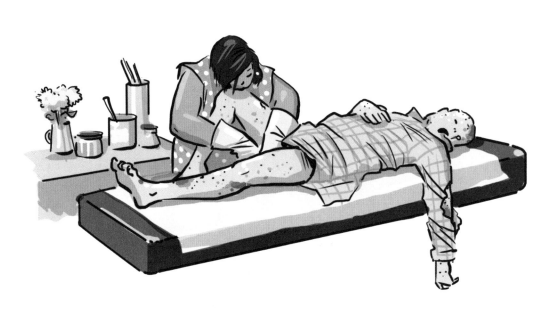

#52: Black Friday

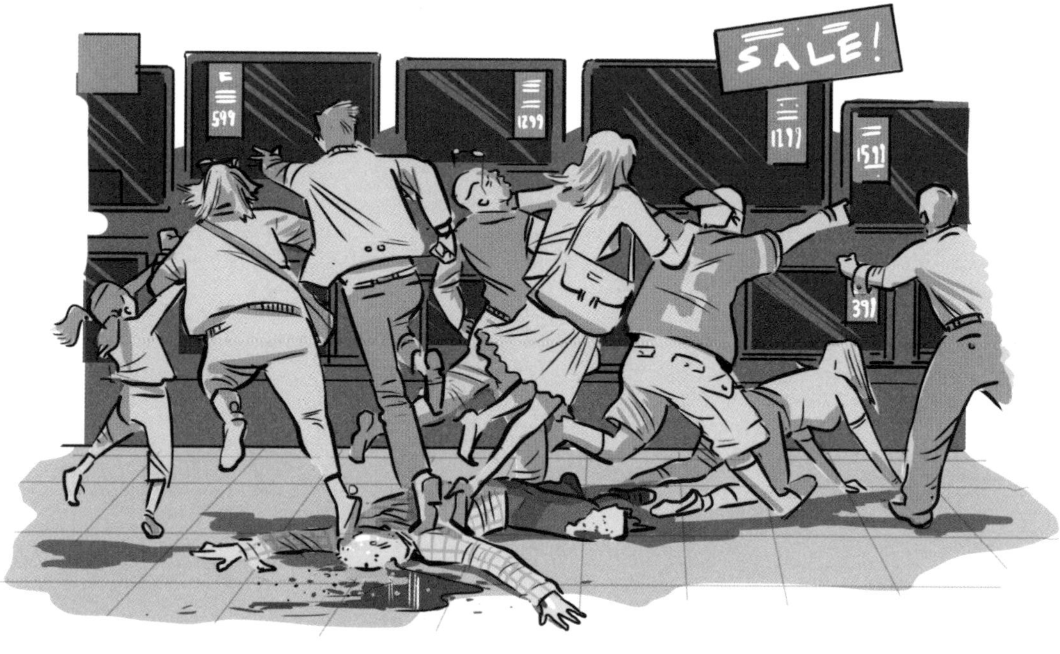
SALE!
599
1299
1199
1599
399

#53: Mythologically

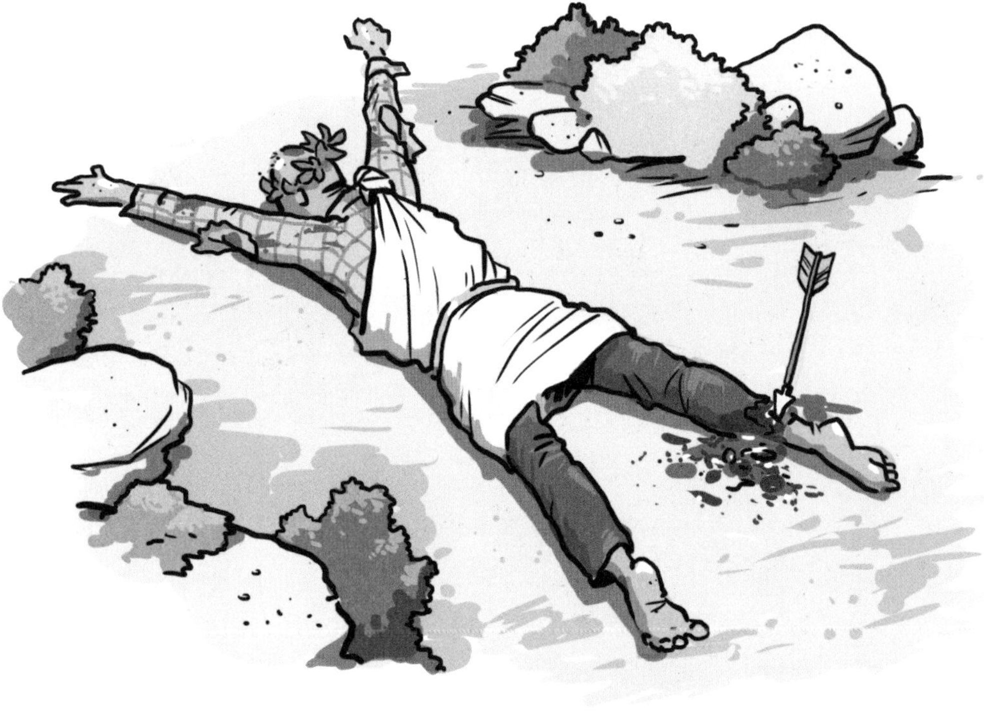

#54: Operatically

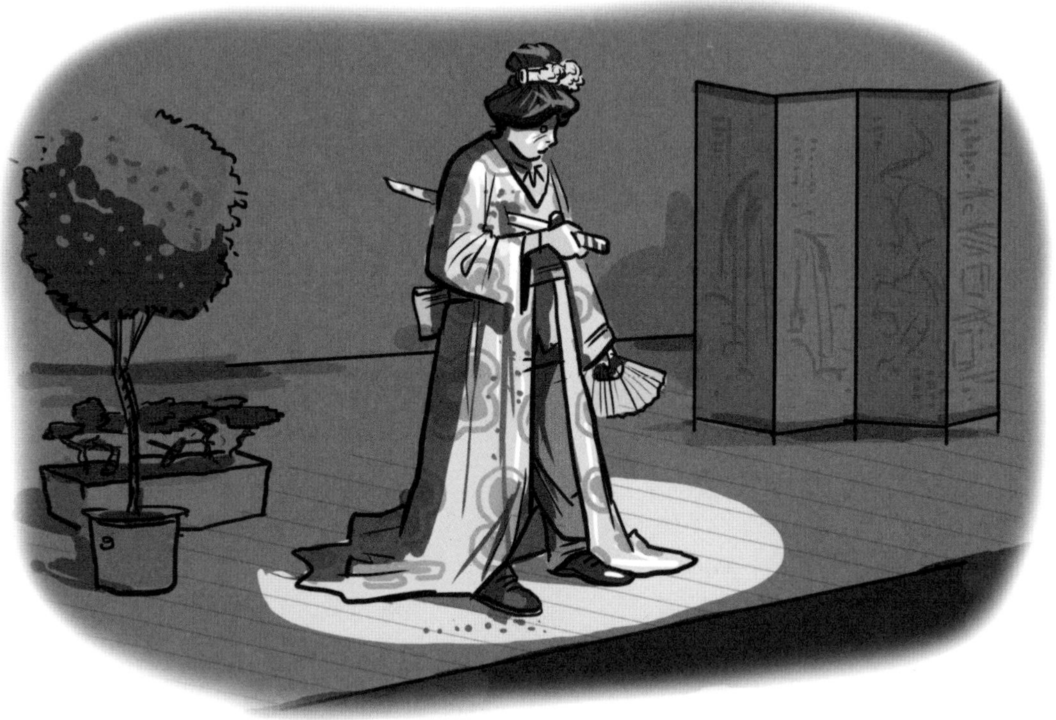

#55: Grand Ole Opry

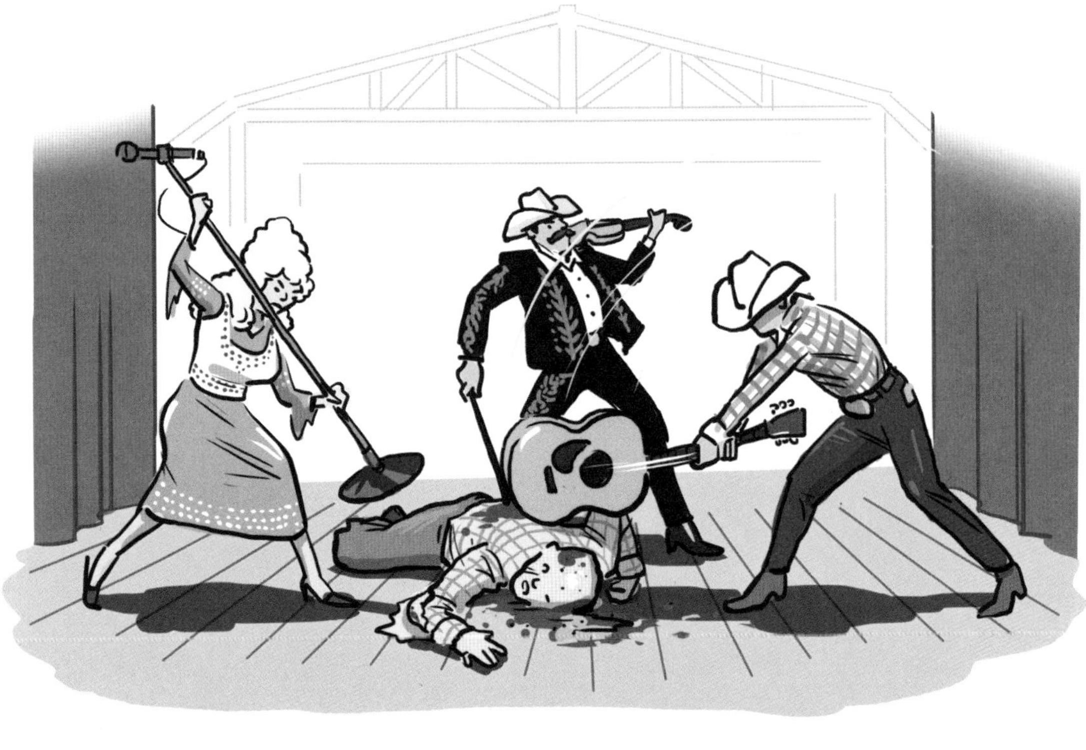

#56: Olde Timey-like

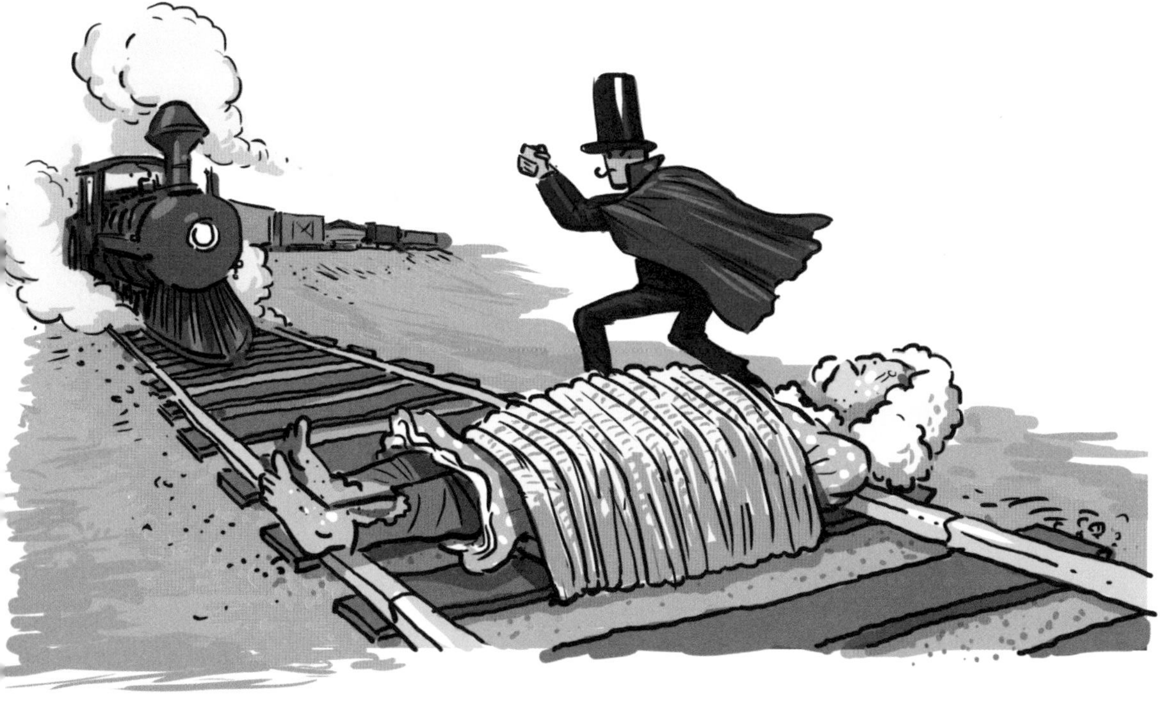

#57: Toilet Paper

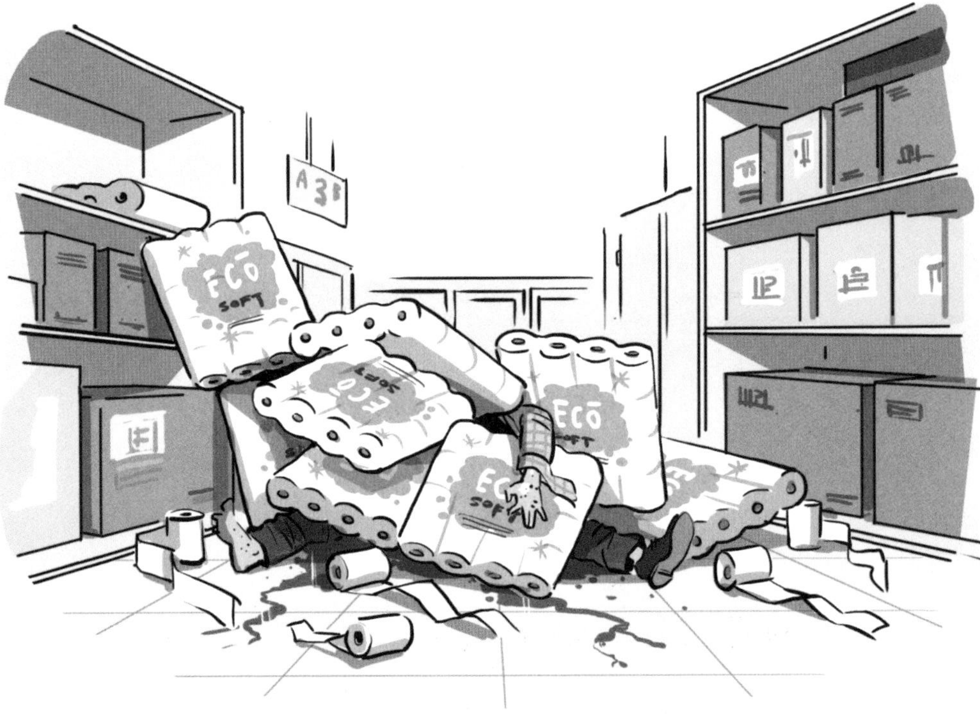
A 3 B
ECO
SOFT
ECO
SOFT

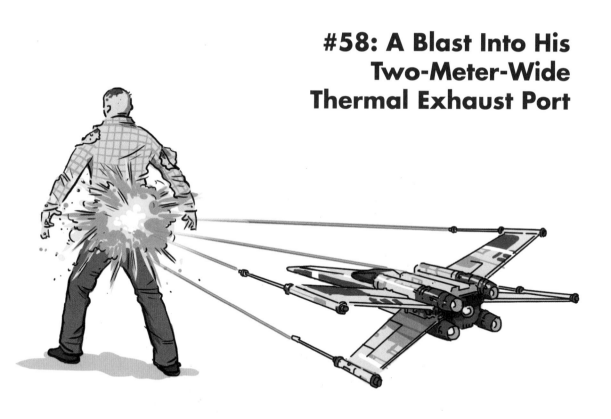

#58: A Blast Into His Two-Meter-Wide Thermal Exhaust Port

#59: Sharks

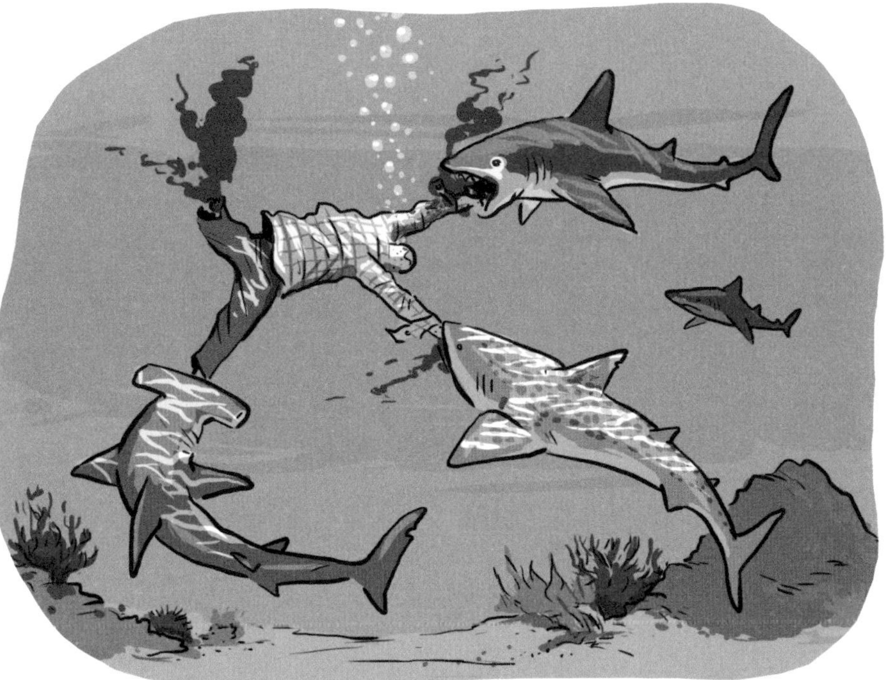

#60: Red Shirt

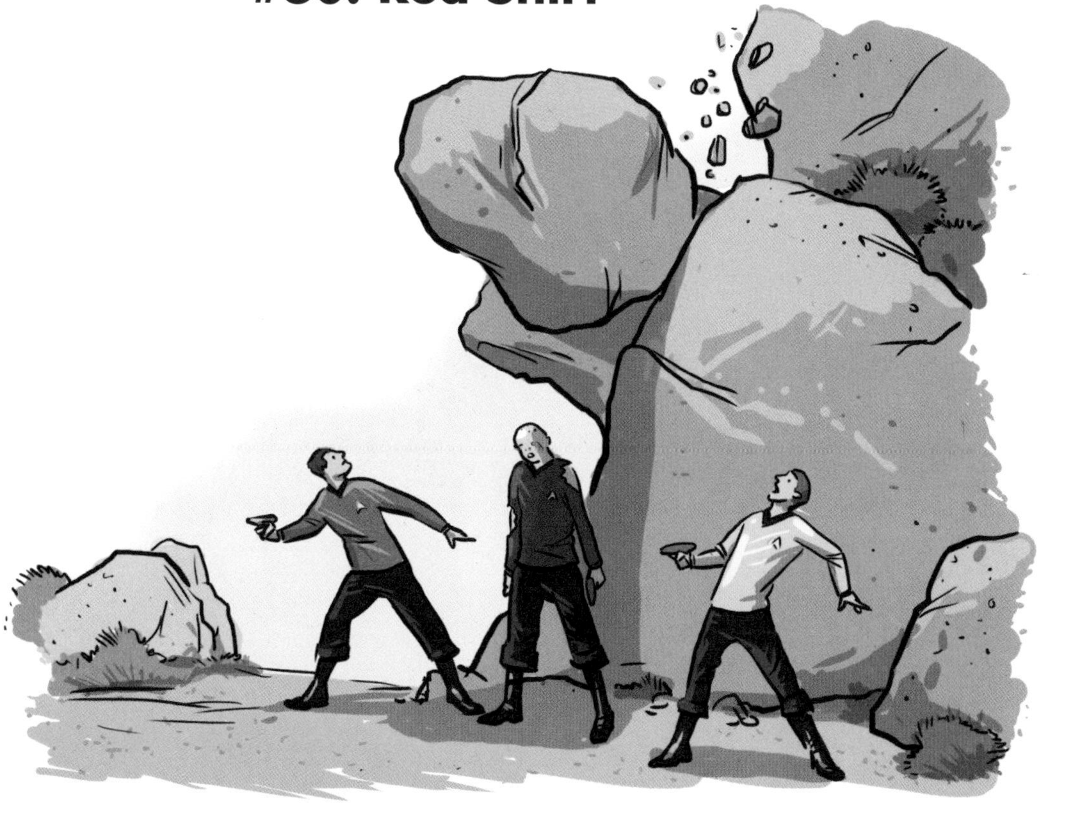

#61: Karate

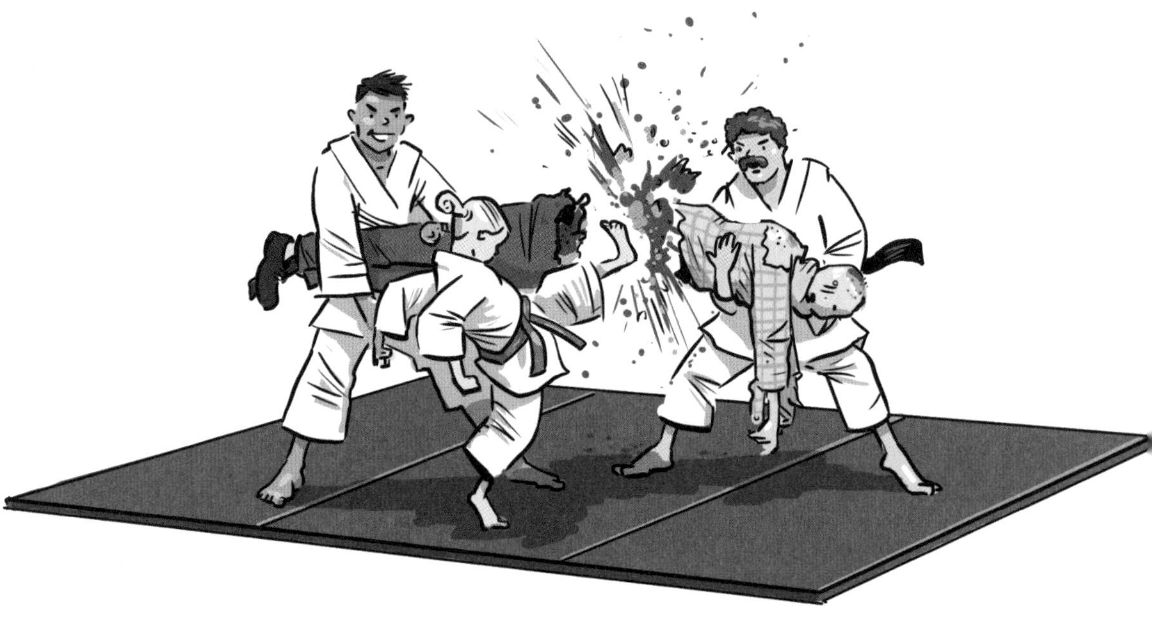

#62: Unicorn

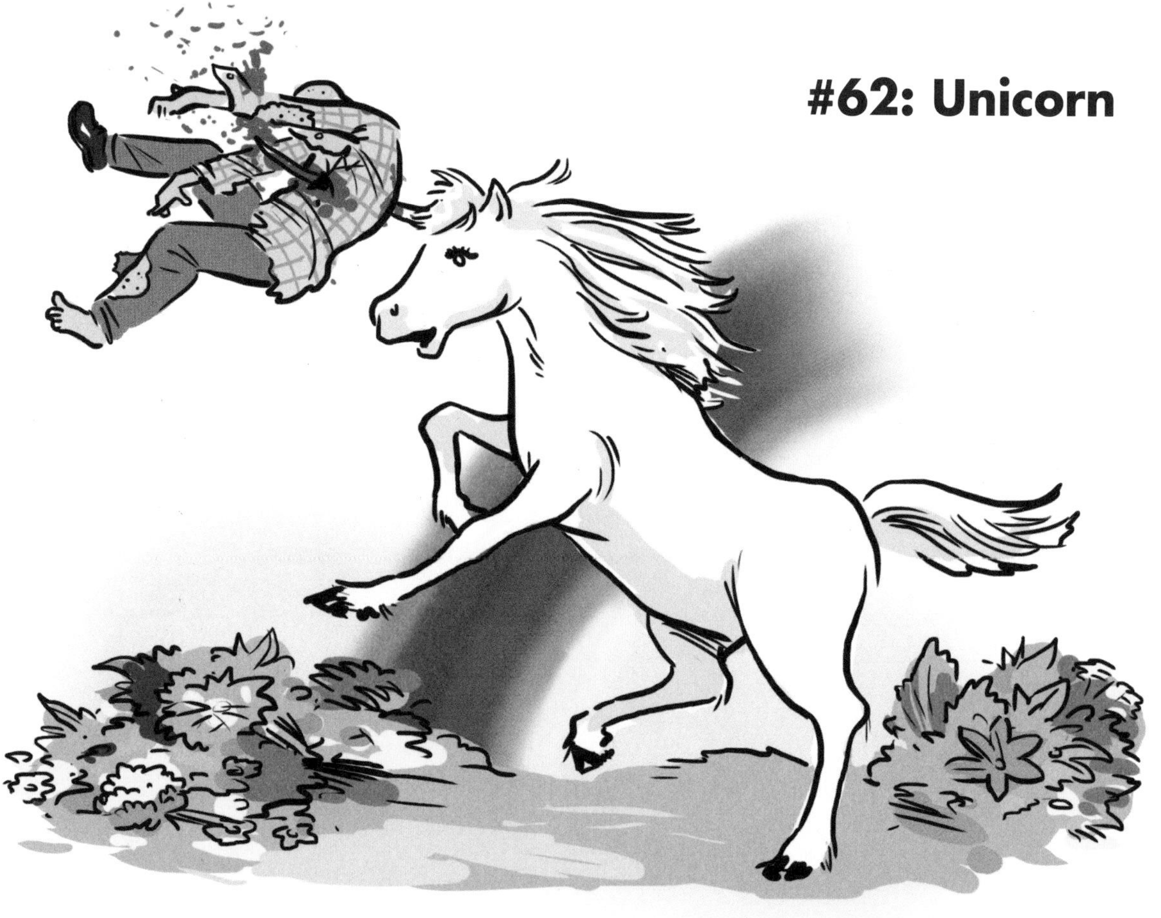

#63: Horse

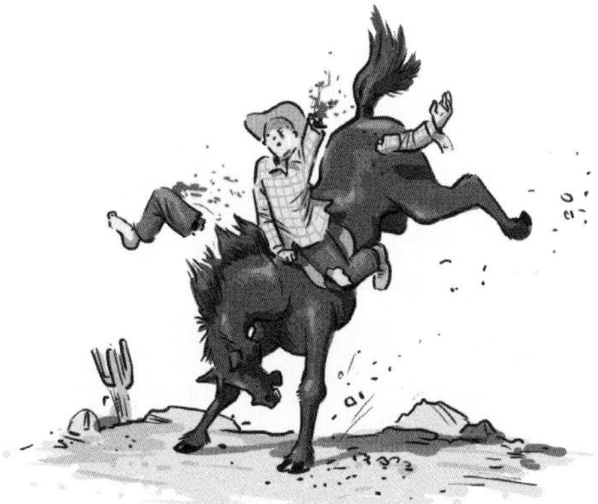

#64: Trojan Horse

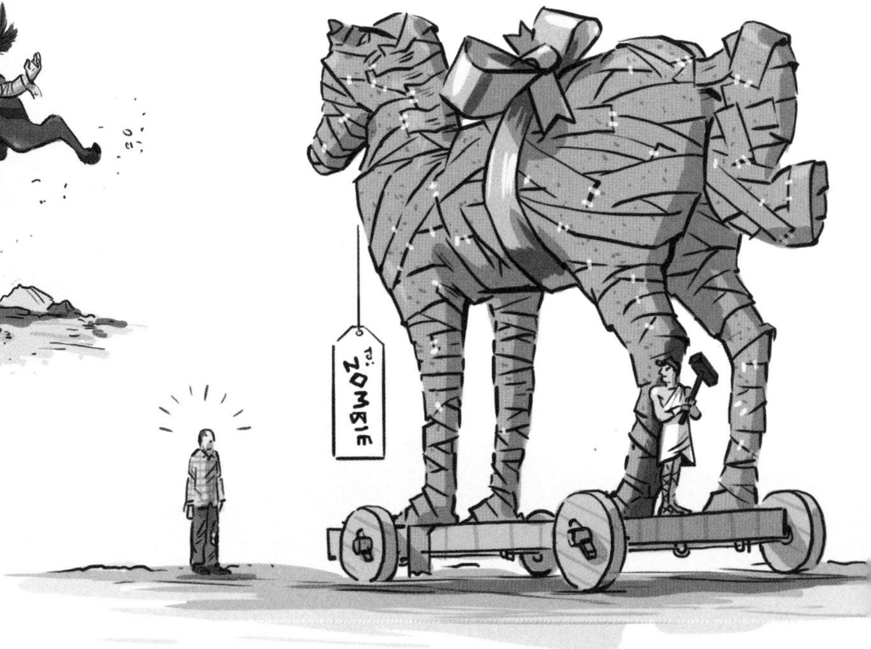
TO: ZOMBIE

#65: Hangman

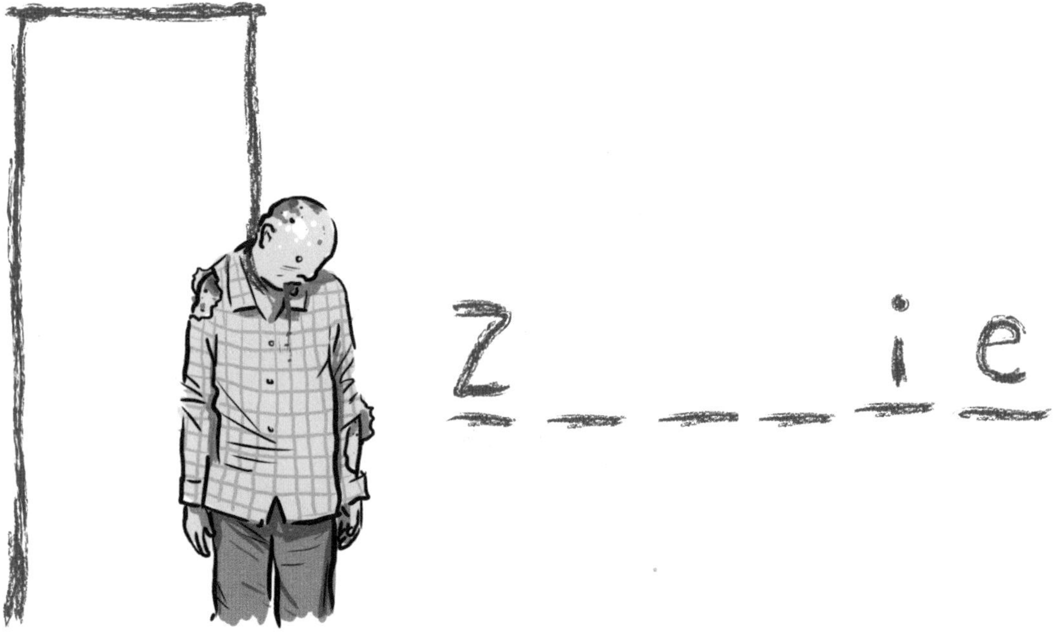
Z _ _ _ i e

#66: Running of the Bulls

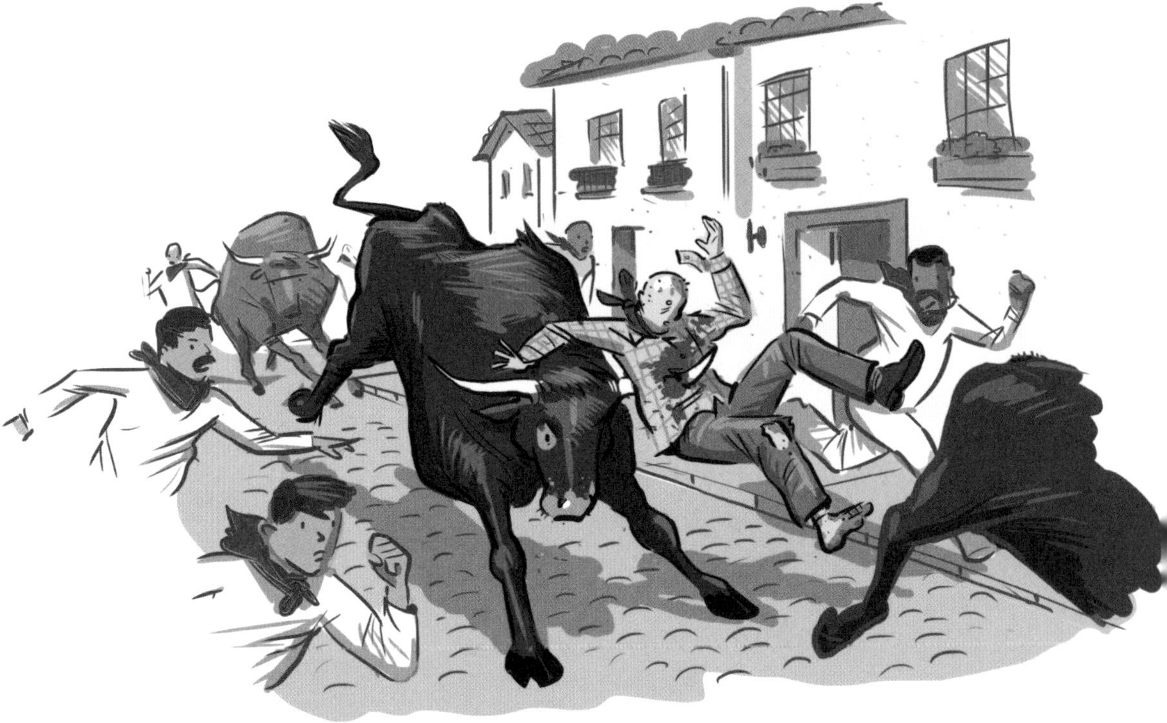

#67: Running of the Brides

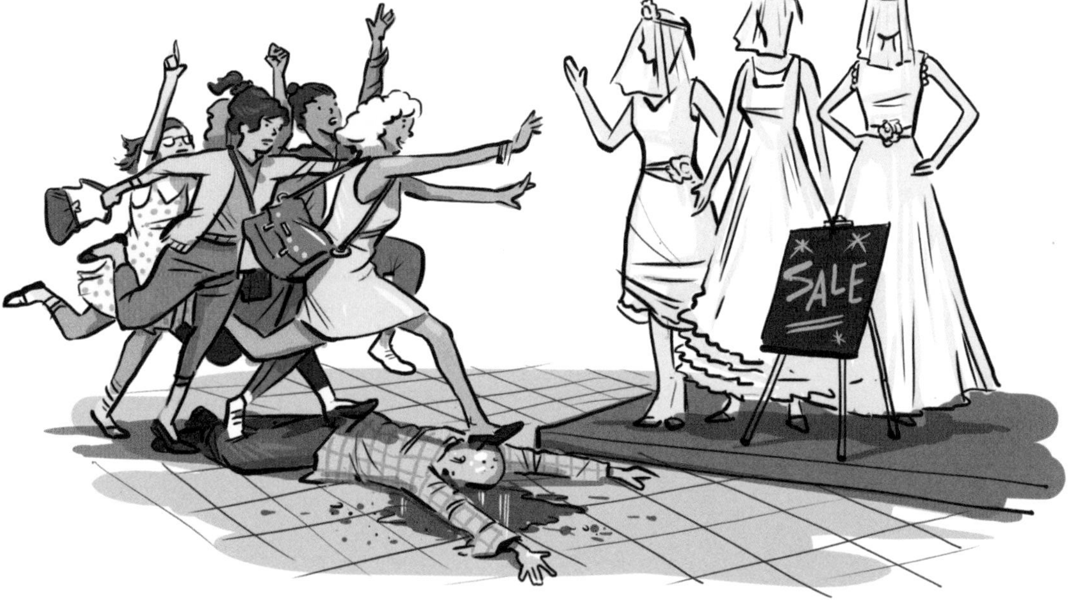
SALE

#68: Running with Scissors

**#69:
Rock
Paper
Scissors**

**#70:
Duck
Duck
Goose**

#71: Humpty Dumpting

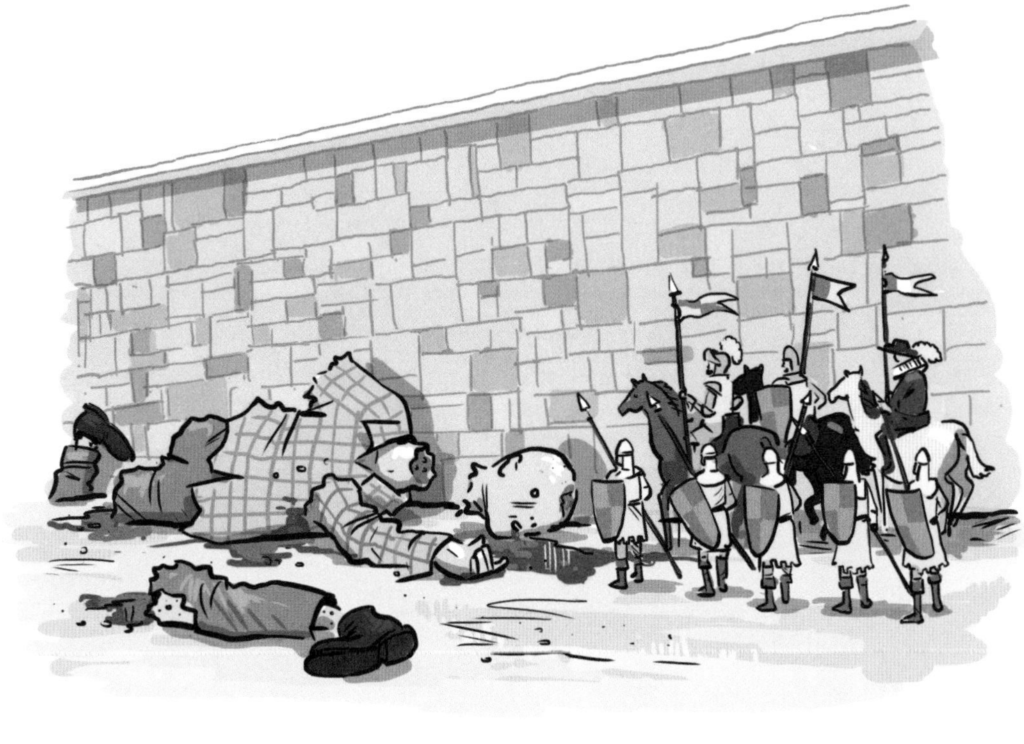

#72: Goldilocksing

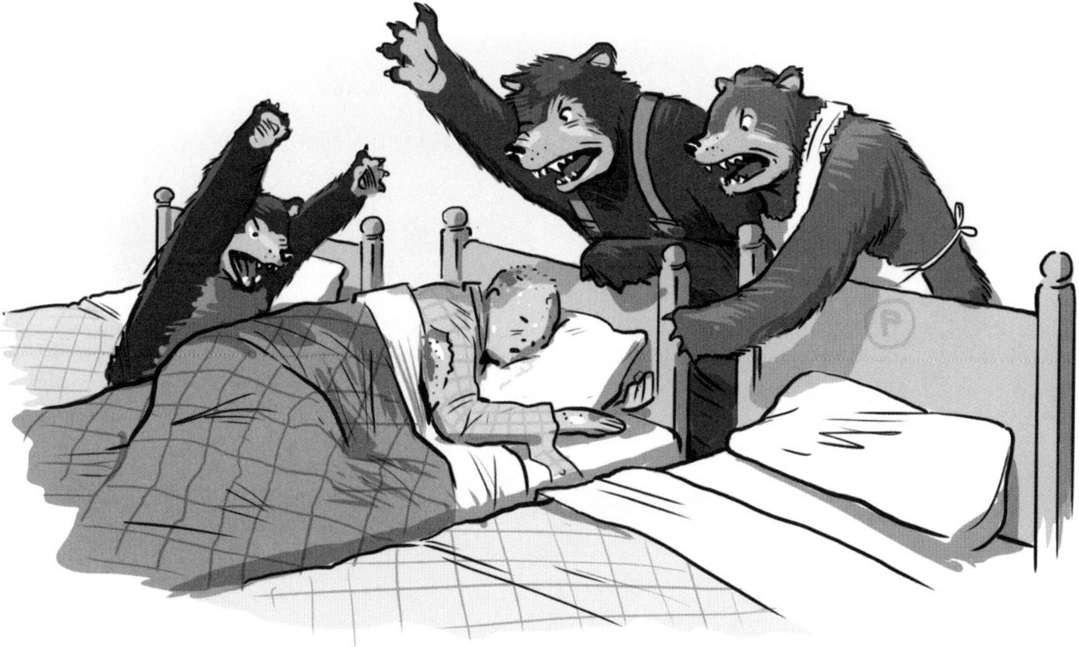

#73: Big Bad Wolf

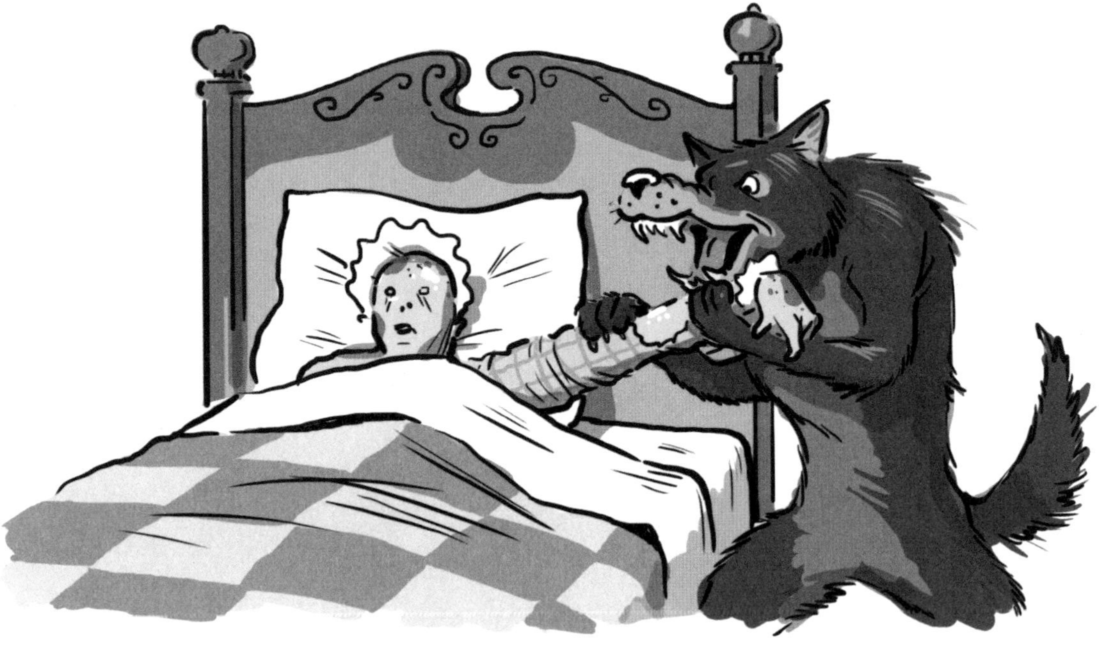

#74: Shakespearean

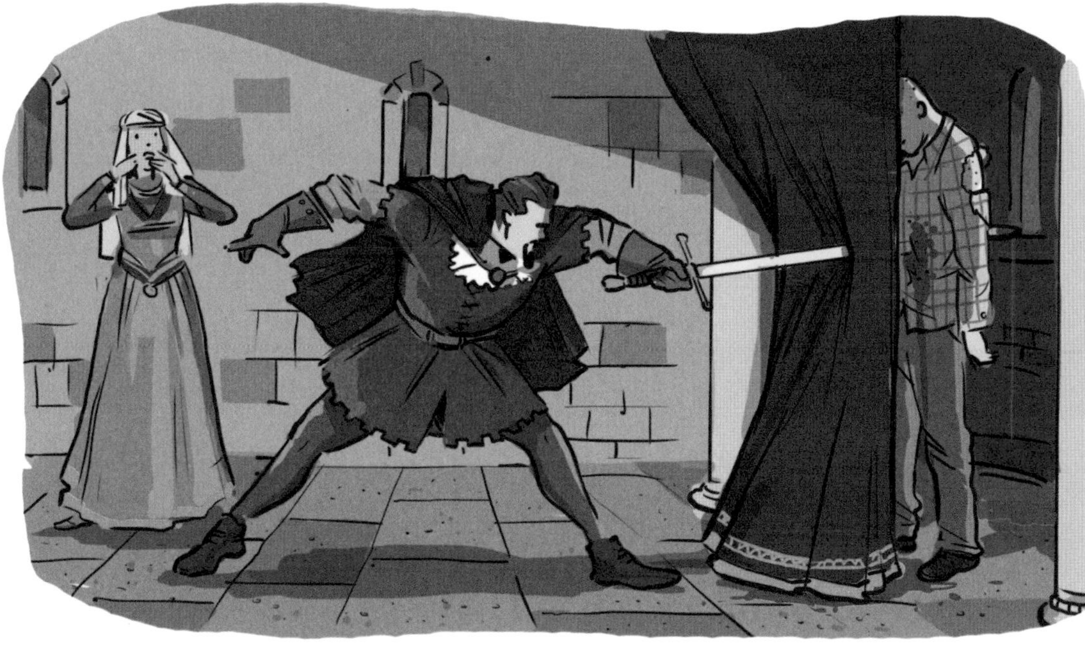

#75: Death by Chocolate

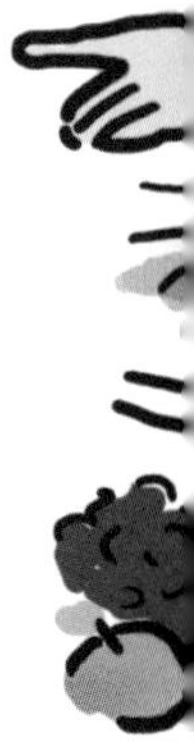

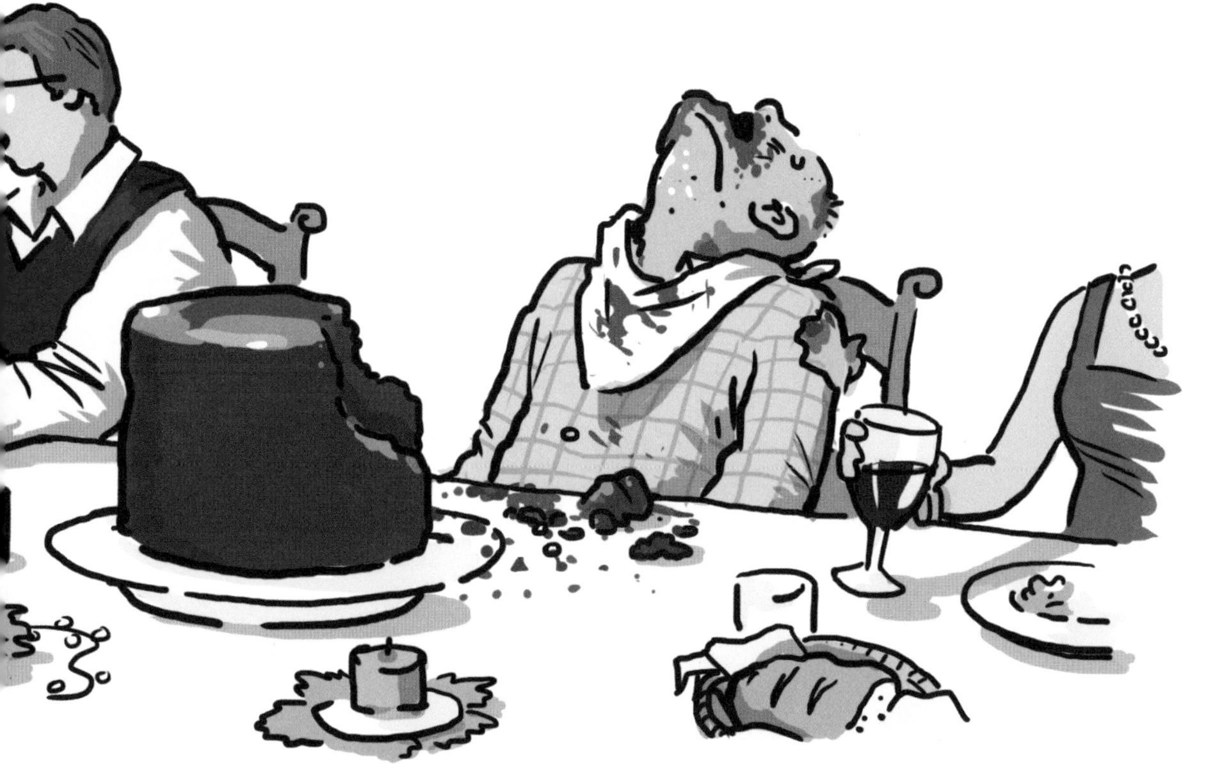

#76: Avada Kedavra

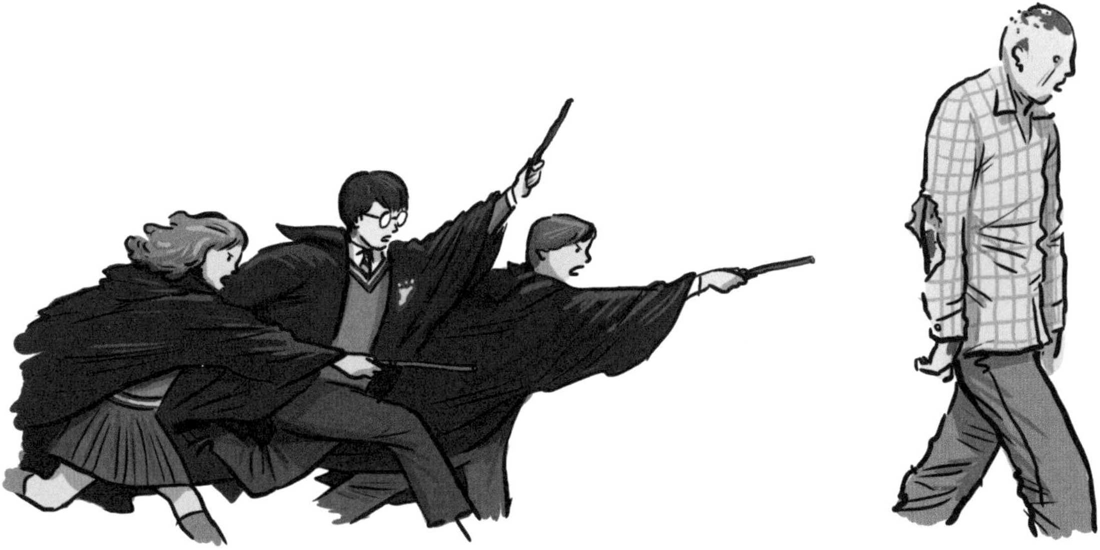

#77: Inigo Montoya

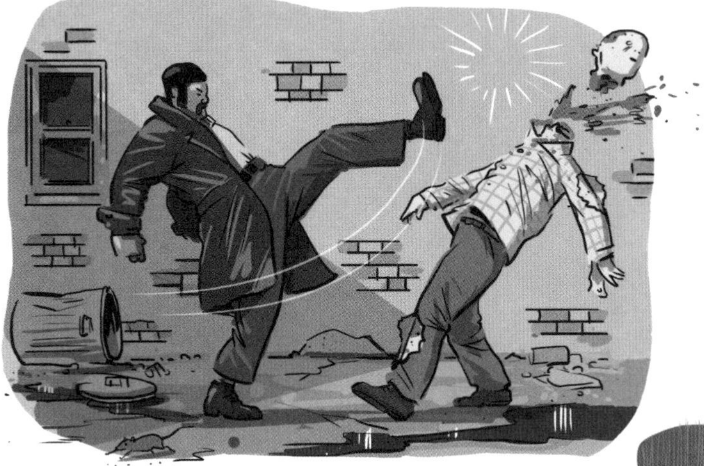

#78: Shaft

#79: Elevator Shaft

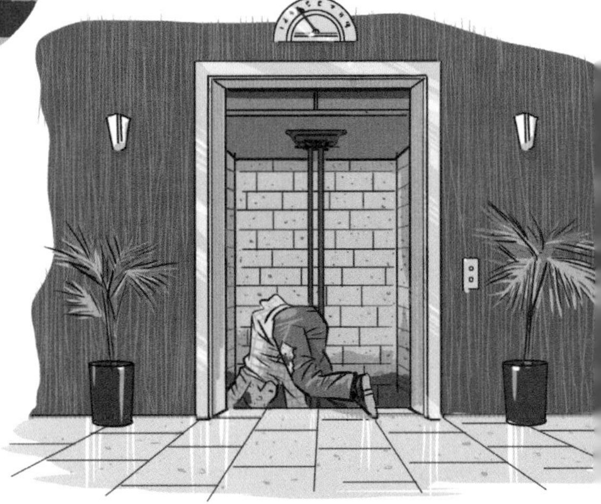

#80: Internship

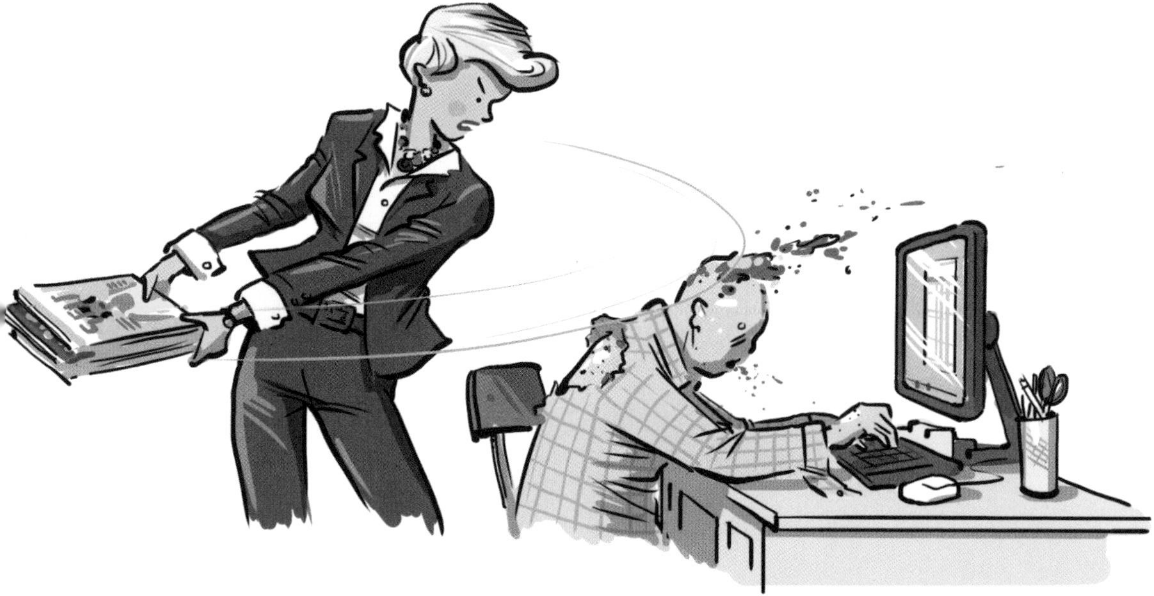

#81: Pillow Fight

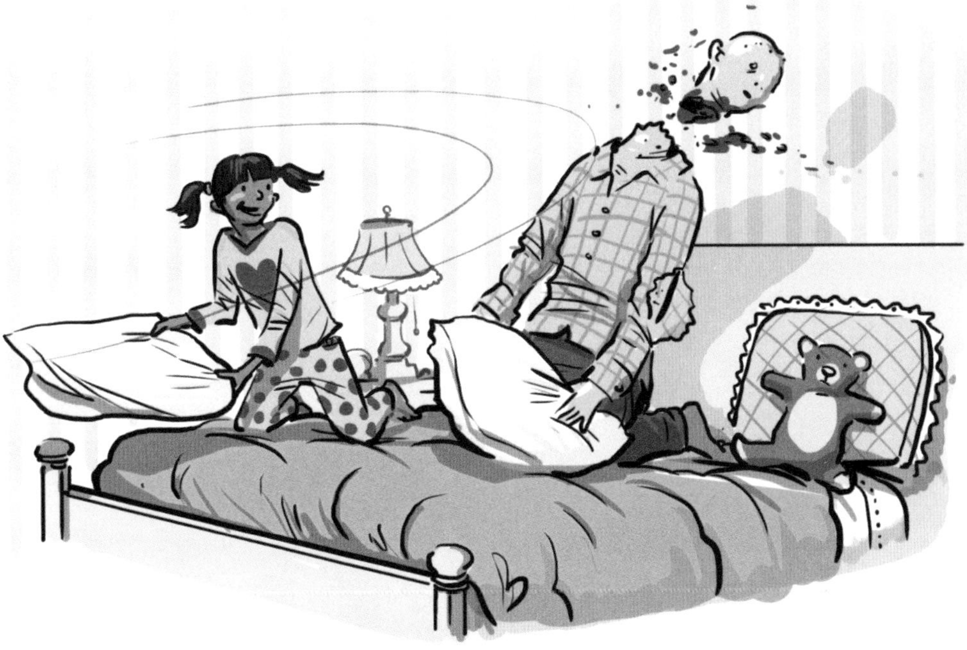

#82: Drone Strike

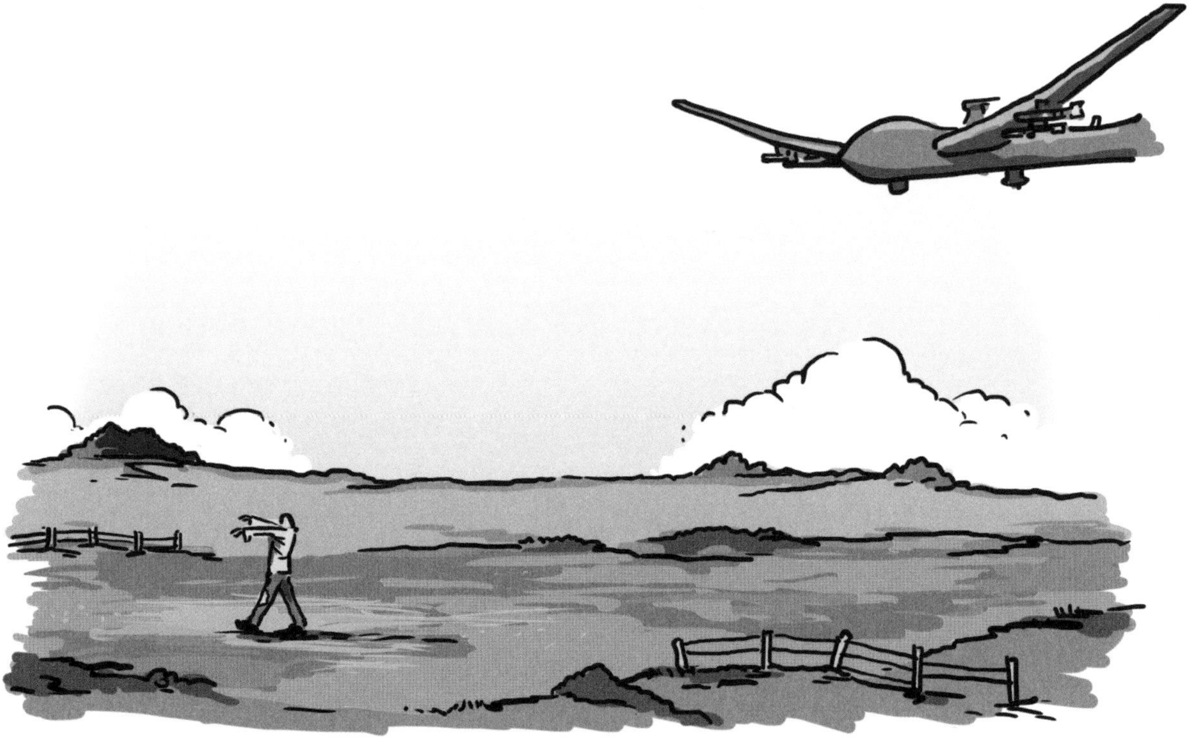

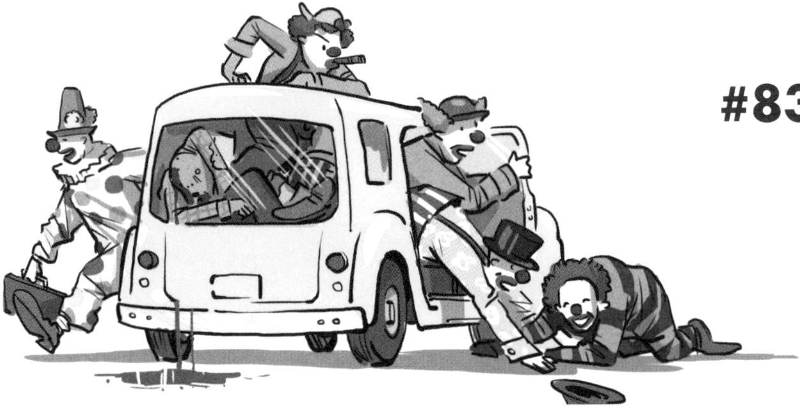

#83: Clown Car

#84: Sewer Clown

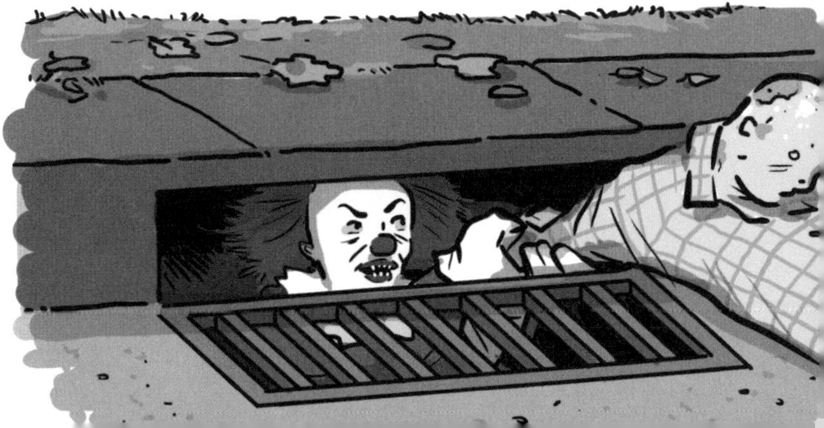

#85: Skydiving

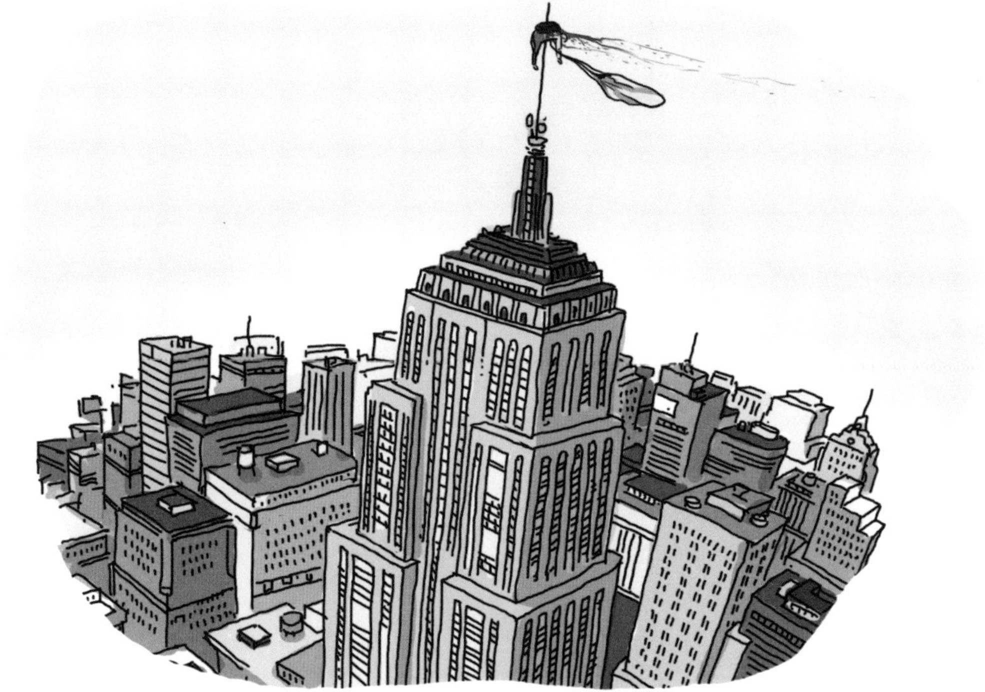

#86: TSA

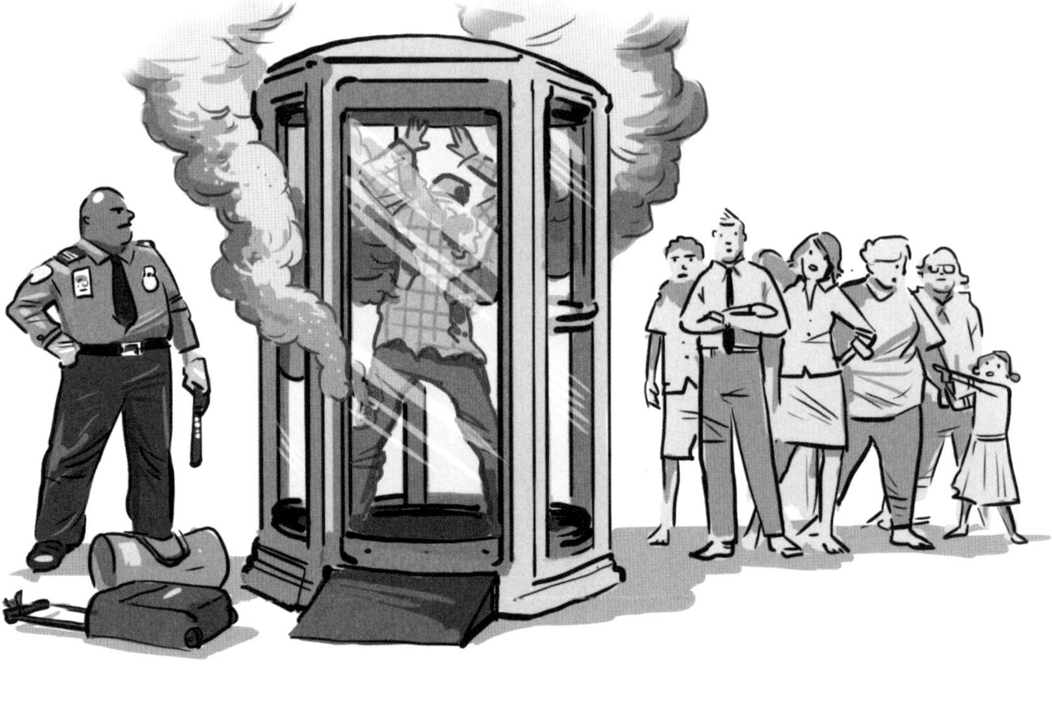

#87: Large Sugary Drinks

#88: Robot Uprising

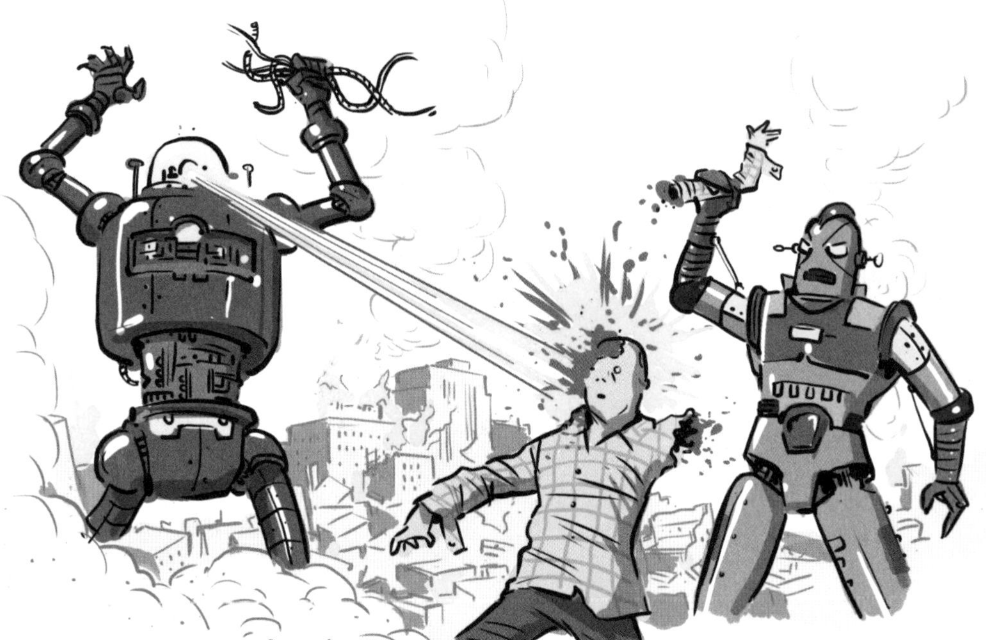

#89: Yoga

#90: Mob Hit (Take the Cannoli)

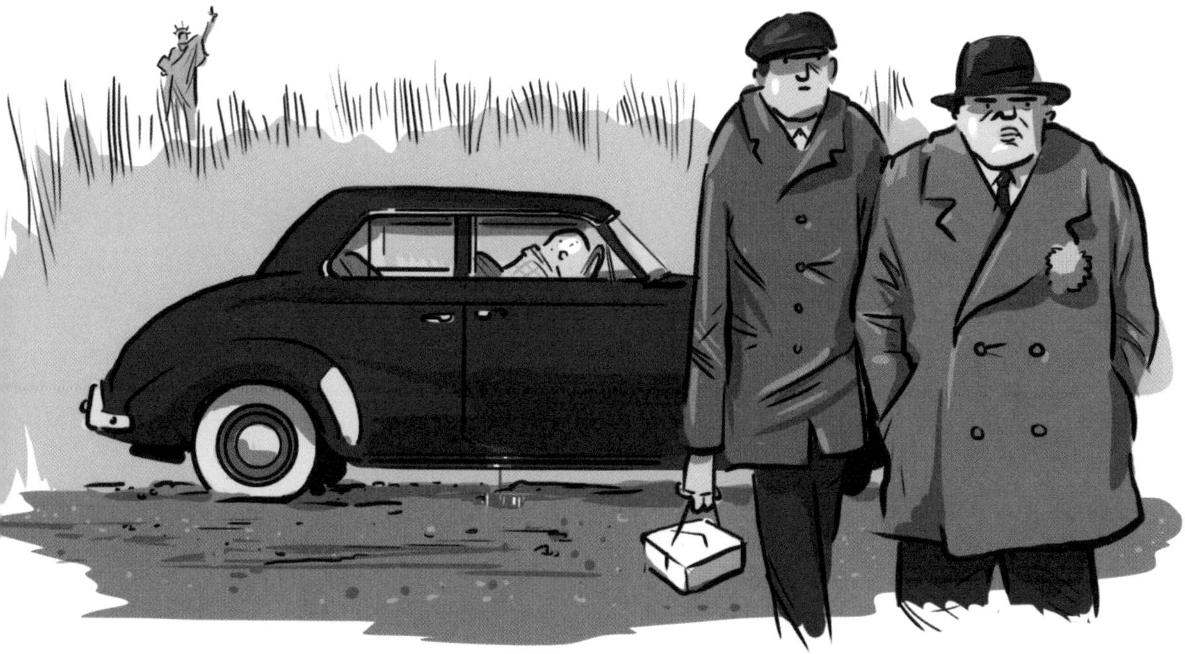

#91: Bieber Fever

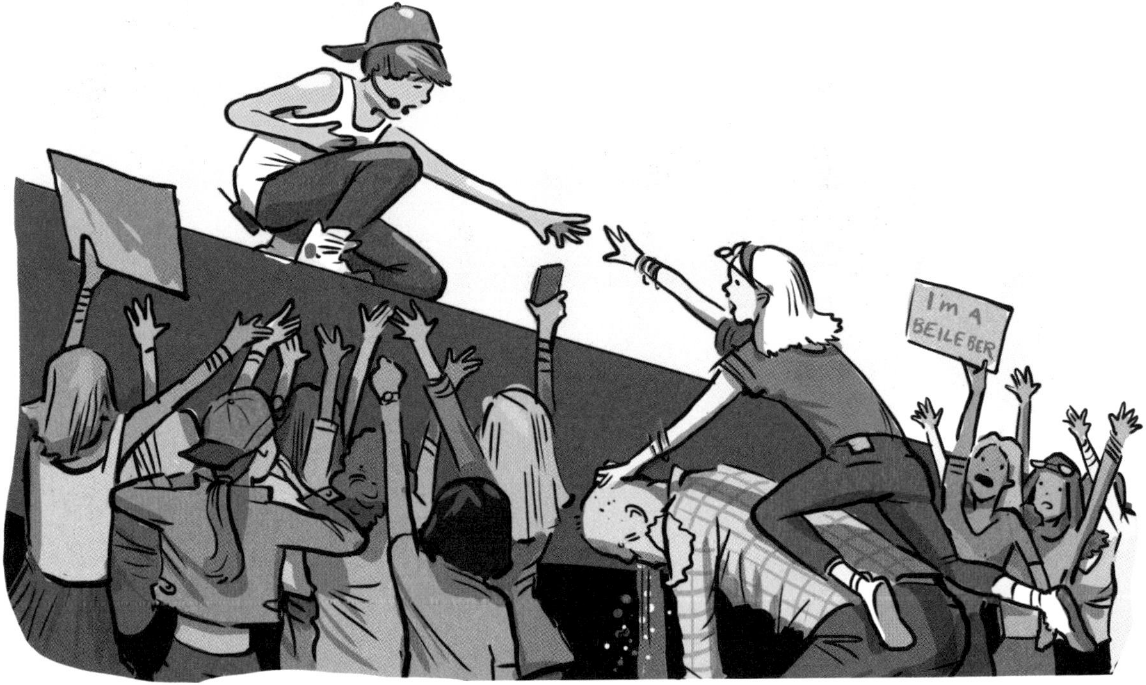
I'm A BEILEBER

#92: Bangs

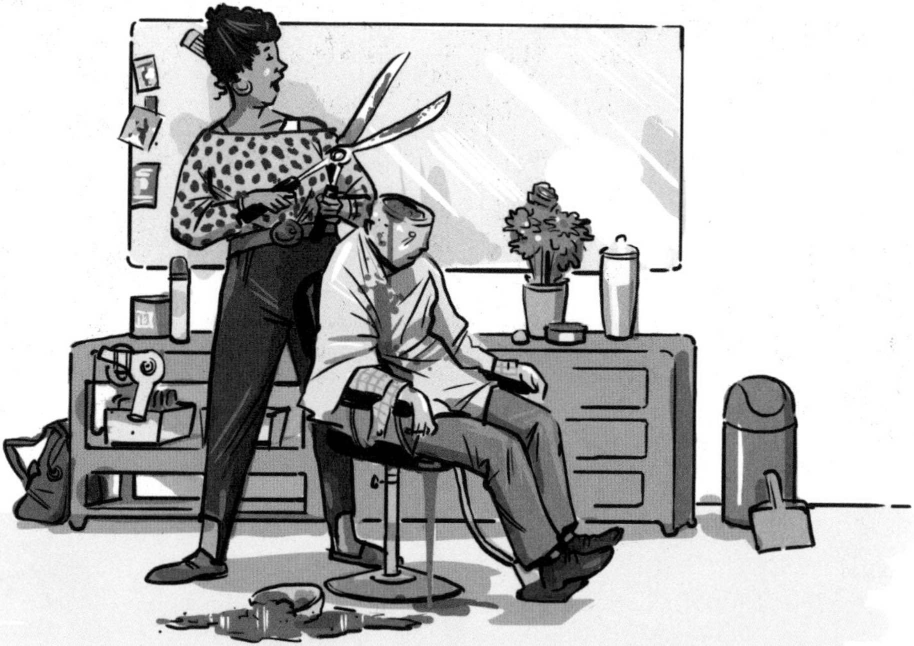

#93: Halloween Party

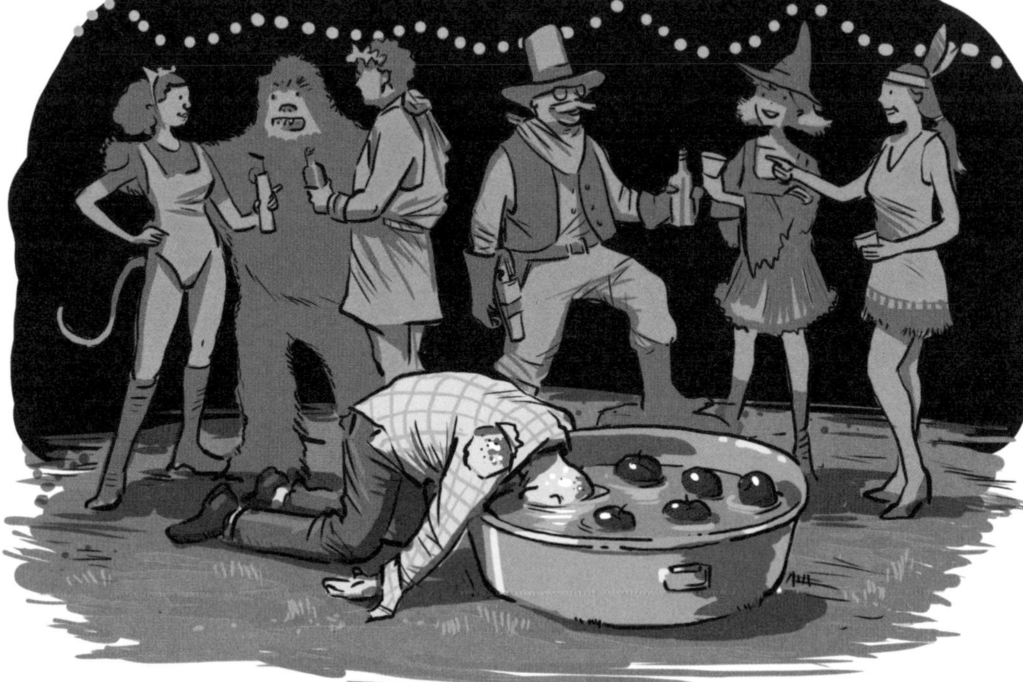

#94: Pumpkin Carving Contest

#95: Paintball

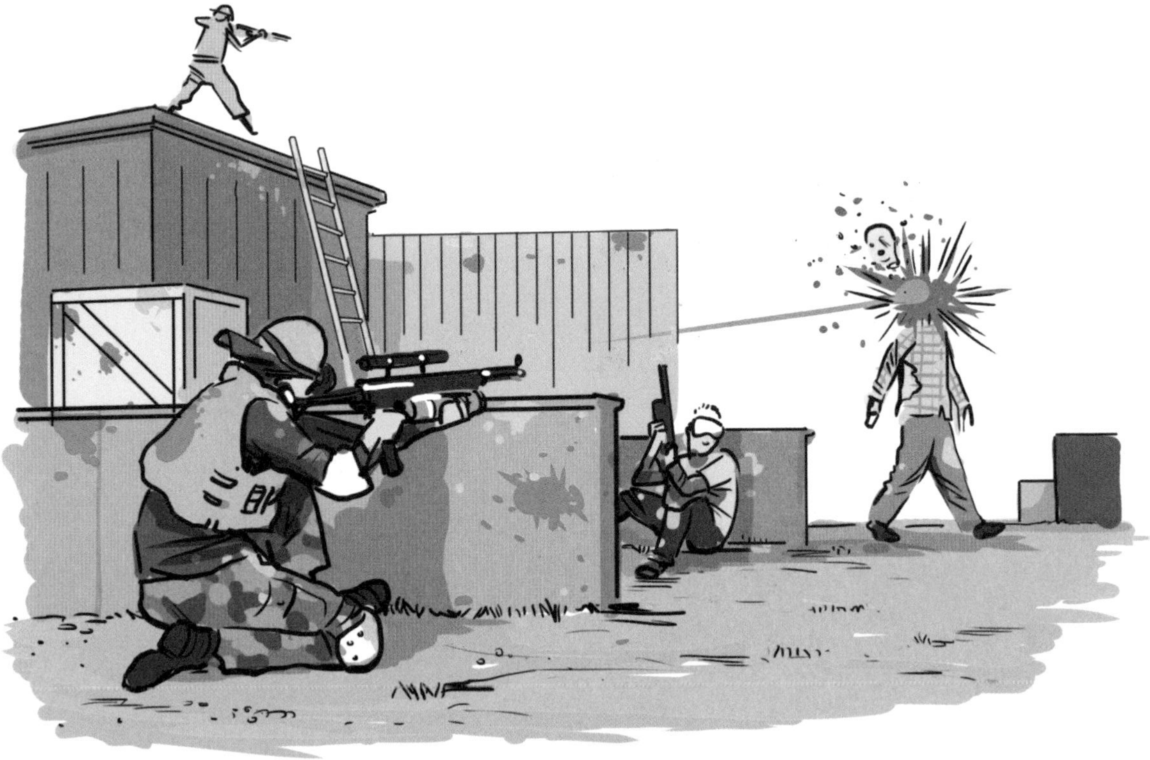

#96: Tailgaiting

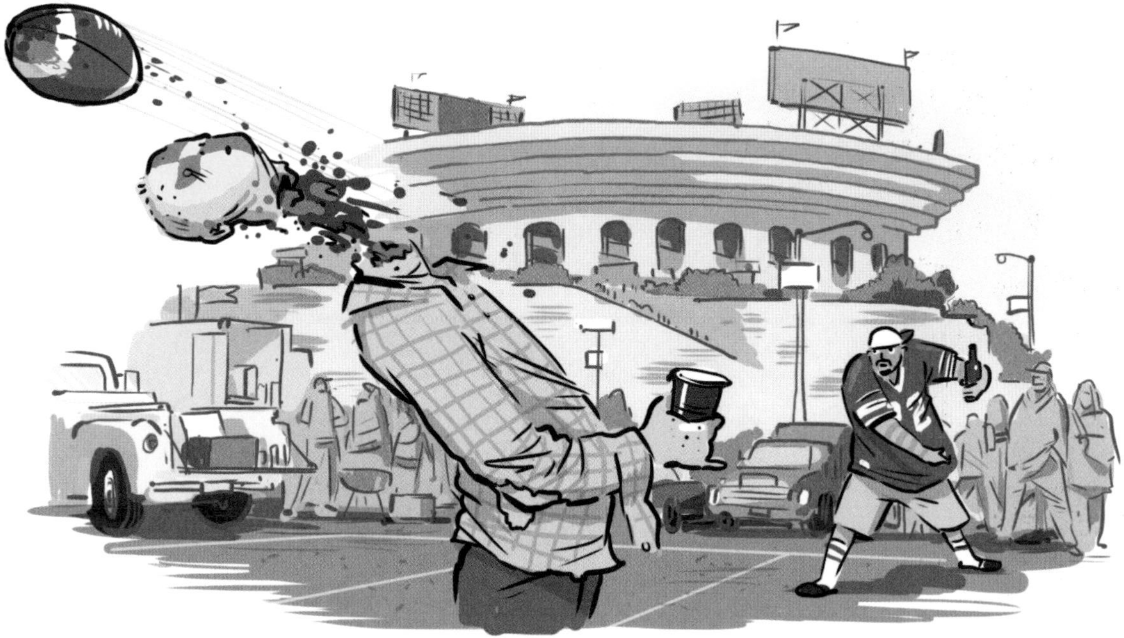

#97: Gallagher

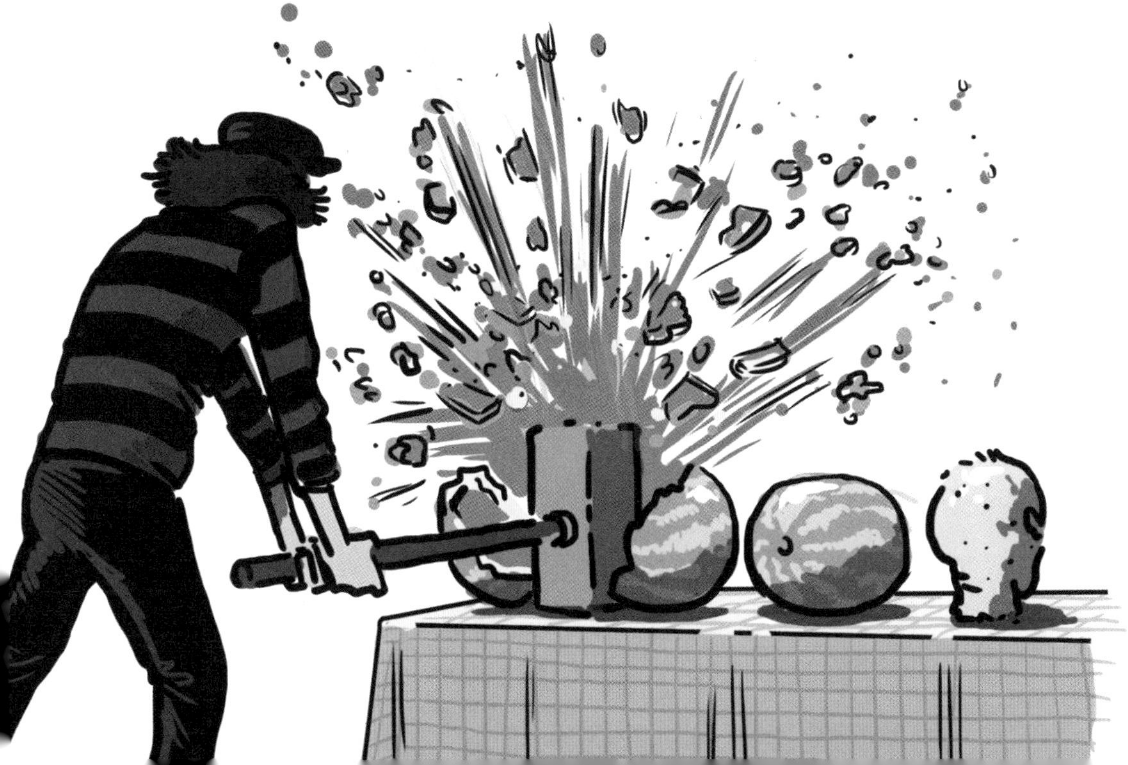

#98: Pre-Morning Coffee Chit Chat

#99: Cuteness Overload

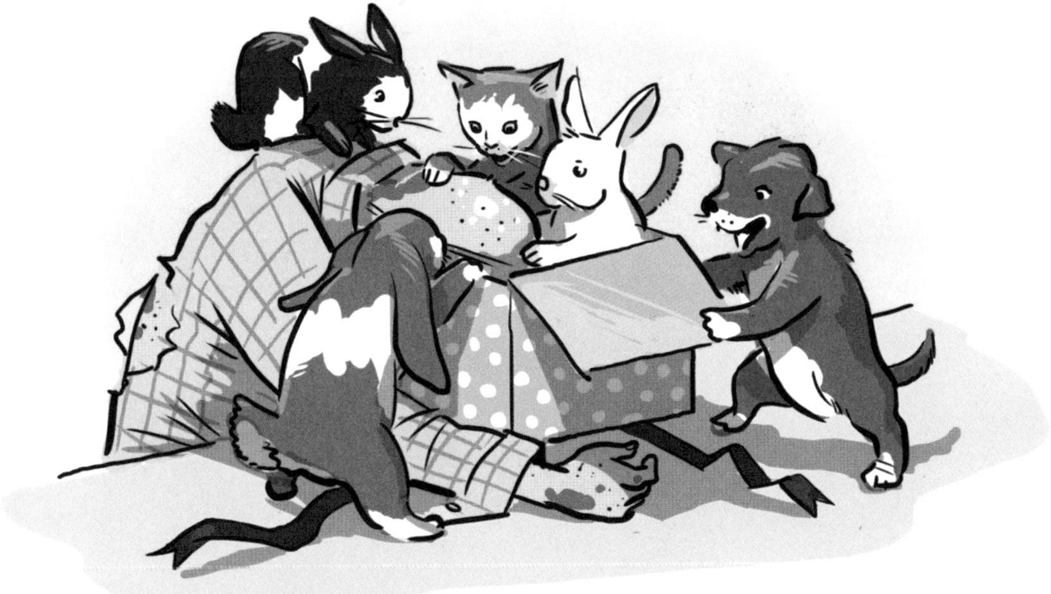

#100: In the Library, With a Candlestick

#101: Google Maps

23rd St
W 24th St
Jemmy's
Dog Run
28 St [6]
New York
Merchandise
Mart Plaza
E 30th St
E 29th St
E 28th St
E 27th St
W 23rd St
Madison Ave
Park Ave S
E 26th St
3rd Ave
2nd Ave
W 22nd St
5th Ave
23 St [N,R]
E 25th St
W 21st St
A
E 23rd St
Lexington Ave
Hype Gym
W 20th St
Fifth Ave
E 26th St
Bellevue
South Par
Broadway
E 25th St
W 19th St
5th Ave
American
Dream Hostel
E 21st St
E 23rd St
E 26th St
18th St
Hotel Verite
E 20th
E 24th St
Uptown
Housing Office
E 22nd St
3rd Ave
2nd Ave
C Von Heyl
E 18th St
Gramercy
Park
E 23rd St
E 24th St
E 17th St
Broadway
E 19th
E 21st St
Fifth Ave
Union Square W
Irving Pl
E 20th St
2nd Ave
E 22nd St
E 15th St
E 16th St
E 17th St
E 18th St
14 St - Union
Sq [N,Q,R]
E 16th St
Simon Baruch
Map data © 2013 Google, Sanborn

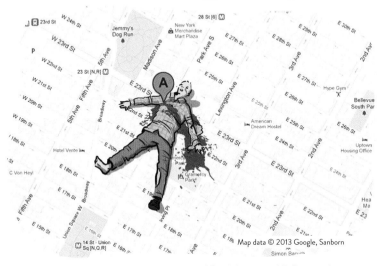

Published by Universe Publishing, a division of Rizzoli International Publications, Inc.
300 Park Avenue South • New York, NY 10010 • www.rizzoliusa.com

2013 2014 2015 2016 2017 / 10 9 8 7 6 5 4 3 2 1

Design: Kayleigh Jankowski • Editor: Jessica Fuller

Printed in the United States • ISBN-13: 978-0-7893-2483-2 • Library of Congress Catalog Control Number: 2013943840